WHO'S IN CHARGE OF YOUR CAREER?
Creating a Strategy for Success

SHERYL SOOKMAN SCHELTER

ISBN: 1-4392-1943-5
ISBN-13: 9781439219430

Visit www.booksurge.com to order additional copies.

TABLE OF CONTENTS

ACKNOWLEDGMENTS

The concept for this book began about eighteen months ago. I decided it was time to create a resource for people that gathered all of the concepts and suggestions I've offered at industry conferences, during Webinars, and in the Career Forum column I've written since 1994 for Meetings Media magazines *(Meetings West, Meetings South, Meetings East, and Meetings Mid-America)*. I had no idea what it would take to complete this book, and I'm so grateful to my family and friends who encouraged me to take my writing to this next level. To my dearest friend, Rachelle Owen, who knows what it's like to follow your dreams. As Dara Torres, the Olympic medal winner, recently said after winning a silver medal at the age of forty-one, "You're never too old to follow your dreams." I'm also grateful to my good friend Kris Wiley and my son Jesse Schmechel for their keen editing skills. To my husband, Fred Schelter, for his ongoing support and love through this process—you'll get your 10 percent someday!

Writing this book is part of the new direction I want my career to take, and I hope the information contained in it will help you find your direction as well.

INTRODUCTION

Since 1994, I've worked with over two thousand people who are either seeking a new position or wanting to make a career change. These individuals are in various stages of their career—some are just starting out in the meetings industry while others have been in the field five, ten, or in some cases more than twenty years. Whether they're seasoned professionals or just entering the industry, they all have something in common—they're unclear about where they want to go next with their careers.

What I've seen is that a vast majority of people tend to keep moving from job to job without any specific focus or direction. Although there might not be gaps in their work histories, their resumes look like a patchwork of disconnected jobs.

With individuals who've reached a senior level position, the disconnect is of a more personal nature. While each job may have given them expanded responsibilities, these individuals are dissatisfied with the direction their career has taken them as well as the skills and experience acquired along the way.

What these individuals lacked was a strategy for success. Once they created a career strategy, they were able to identify what's important to them in terms of their personal interests and priorities, as well as their professional goals. As a result, they began making better assessments about job opportunities.

The process starts with putting together a Wish List and a Preference List. These help you identify your interests, priorities, and goals. Once you've done this, the next step is to develop a Plan of Action, what I refer to as your Personal Marketing Plan. This is how you'll get yourself from your current to your future job.

Taking a new job without knowing if it really fits with your professional goals and personal priorities is like walking around in a fog. You're moving around but you're not exactly sure where you're going or if the next step you take will head you into a brick wall. By creating a career strategy, you're able to figure out where you want to go and how you plan to get there.

Here's another way of looking at it. Let's say you decide to go on a hike. Before you do, there are a number of factors to consider.

You'll need to:

1) Decide where you want to go on your hike
2) Evaluate the level of difficulty of the hike (does it match your physical capabilities?)
3) Determine if you'll need any special pieces of equipment or additional training
4) Figure out how long it will take to complete the hike
5) Get a map so you don't get lost

What you're doing is creating a Plan of Action so you make this hike a success. It's the same thing with your career—you need a Plan of Action to you make your goal a reality.

Once you've clearly defined your strategy, you'll want to build a resume that reflects your career goals. The primary piece you have to market yourself is your resume because it's the first thing prospective employers see that gets them interested in you as a potential candidate. The final chapters of this book focus on the process of creating a resume that clearly communicates your accomplishments and experience and grabs the reader's attention. You'll also find tips for creating a resume that passes the electronic screening process.

It's up to you to decide where you want your career to head and then develop a strategy so you can make it happen. While the opportunities you receive impact the level of success and time it takes to achieve your goal, you can help drive the process with the relationships you develop along the way.

This book will take you step-by-step through the process so you can create a career strategy that matches your personal and professional goals.

Chapter One

FIND YOUR YELLOW
BRICK ROAD

The path you're about to start on is like the yellow brick road that Dorothy took in her adventures in the Land of Oz. Although there are lots of unknowns as you begin the process, with a little work on your part, there's sure to be a treasure at the end that's worth pursuing.

The first step in creating a career strategy is to make a list of things you enjoy doing or wish you had the time to do. Do you remember when you were a kid and someone would ask what you wanted to be or do when you grew up? At that point, the sky was the limit and nothing was too ridiculous to consider. You want to take the same approach at this stage of the process—everything is possible.

Is there a subject you're interested in learning more about? Is there something happening in your community, nationally, or globally that you're interested in helping to improve or change? Do you have a hobby that gives you a lot of pleasure, or is there one you used to enjoy but haven't been able to dedicate time to for a while?

In *Don't Sweat the Small Stuff*, author Richard Carlson offers simple ways to put some of life's daily changes into perspective. I keep one of his messages in my office to remind me who's in charge of what's happening in my life. It says, "Life, like an automobile, is driven from the inside out, not the other way." As you begin putting your Wish List together, remember not to eliminate things in advance because of concerns or objections your family, friends, or coworkers may have. While there may be factors you need to take into consideration when you assess your career strategy, remember that you're the one in charge of the direction you want your career to take.

Step One – Put Together Your Wish List

Your Wish List contains two sections—your personal and professional interests. This is your Wish List, so don't hesitate to put anything on there that you've done before and "wished" you had more time to do again, or something that you "wish" you could learn more about. Remember not to pre-edit the things you put on your Wish List.

Column One: Personal

Create a column with all of the things you enjoy doing, whether that's playing golf, going hiking, doing some type of volunteer work, or maybe engaging in some type of craft or art work. Include things on this list that you may not have been able to do for a while because of restrictions with work and/or family obligations. Wouldn't your work be more pleasurable if you could plan meetings and events for a company or organization whose business or service matched with the things you're passionate about?

Column Two: Professional

The items on this list are the things you currently enjoy doing in your job, aspects of your job you wish you had more time to focus on, and areas of work you'd like to gain experience doing.

Maybe you've been coordinating trade shows for a number of years but haven't had the chance to manage them outside of the United States.

Put on your list "Manage international trade shows." If you studied a language in college and always wished you could find a job that involved interfacing with attendees who spoke that language, put down "Use foreign language skills." If you'd like to be involved with the strategic management of meetings at your company or organization, put that on your Wish List (see the sample Wish List on pages 8–10).

Step Two: Don't Be Your Own Worst Enemy

It's critical that you avoid sabotaging yourself with mental roadblocks or obstacles to your own success. If you begin determining in advance that it's impossible to make a change in your career, then stop and analyze the origin of this obstacle. Is it based on facts, is it self-imposed, or does it come from what you believe others will say, i.e., family, friends, coworkers? Henry Ford once said, "Obstacles are those frightful things you see when you take your eyes off your goal." Figure out how to get past this hurdle so you can achieve your career goal.

Step Three: Rank Your Interests

Once you've completed your list of personal and professional interests, it's time to go back and rank them (see the sample Wish List on page 9). This step will help you determine areas where you want to focus your career strategy. You may also find some compatibility with the items in each of the columns.

Example: Susan's personal column includes playing golf and volunteering with nonprofit organizations, while her professional column includes managing golf tournaments. Susan has assisted with coordinating the golf tournament at her current employer's annual sales meeting the last three years. Reviewing her list, Susan realized that what she'd like to do is combine her passion for golf with her experience coordinating tournaments and use them to help nonprofit organizations coordinate their charity golf tournaments. While Susan has helped secure vendors as sponsors for her company's tournament, she's not sure how or whom nonprofits solicit as sponsors. This is the missing skill set she feels is necessary to help her achieve her career goal. The local Habitat for Humanity chapter she volunteers with has an annual golf tournament. Susan plans to get involved with the sponsorship committee this year so she can learn the type of companies they target for sponsors.

Step Four: Additional Skills Needed

Don't worry at this point if items you've included require gaining additional training or education. Maybe your goal is to become the manager of meetings or the vice president of strategic planning for a company or organization. Most senior level positions require at least a bachelor's degree. In addition, many employers now state that candidates must have either the designation of a Certified Meeting Professional (CMP) or Certified Meeting Manager (CMM).

Suppose you identify that becoming a Certified Meeting Manager (CMM) is an important part of your strategy, and your company supports your efforts. In the business plan you put together for your CMM, you decide to focus on a way of improving the meetings process in your department. After receiving your CMM, you present the business plan to your company; not only do they buy off on the concept, they offer you an expanded role and a promotion.

If these certifications give you the upper edge as a candidate, then flag them as Need to Research (NTR) so you can determine what's involved with acquiring these certifications (see the sample Wish List on page 10).

The same holds true for other skills. Maybe you included on your Wish List that you want to learn how to design Web sites or registration databases. You might need to explore different avenues to acquire these types of specific skill sets:

- ✓ Self-learning: Are there books available that would allow you to teach yourself this new skill?
- ✓ Classes: Do any local community colleges or computer training schools offer courses on these subjects?

When you begin investigating the costs for these courses, be sure to investigate all of your resources. Find out if your employer provides tuition reimbursement. Check to see if one of the professional associations you belong to offers any educational support.

Another important thing to take into consideration is how much time it will take to achieve one of these educational goals. To avoid losing time from work, find out if you can attend courses in the evenings or on the weekends.

One other option to explore is acquiring a desired skill through your current job. Investigate opportunities to transfer to another department within the company where you currently work so that you can learn this new skill. Let's say you want to learn the technical aspects of producing general sessions. If your company or organization has its own media production department, you might discuss your goals with the head of the department to find out if you could acquire the skills you desire by working more closely with that department. Maybe you could shadow someone in the department or transfer on a temporary basis.

Example: Martha had been planning meetings and events for over ten years for a telecommunications company. Over time, the area she realized she really enjoyed was the marketing aspects of her programs. She knew that the Marketing Department was creating a campaign for a new product the company was launching. Martha researched the new product and prepared a marketing plan that outlined a number of ways her qualifications could benefit the department and this specific product launch. She arranged a meeting with the vice president of marketing to discuss joining this new team, and he responded favorably to her plan. After the product launch, he invited Martha to transfer permanently to the Marketing Department.

Step Five: Birds of a Feather Flock Together – Pairing Up Your Personal and Professional Lists

Look at your lists to see where there are areas of interest that match or are compatible. Put these matches on a second list called Potential Career Avenues. Use this list to begin refining your career options by doing research to determine different avenues available within these categories.

Example: Francesca has owned a small incentive planning company for over twenty-five years designing high-end programs for her corporate clients to international destinations. Her personal passion is cooking and wine appreciation. Francesca has decided to combine her international travel experience with her love of cooking and is developing a series of customized cooking tours for groups to Europe and South America. She has found a way to blend passion and experience together.

Example: Linda is an avid outdoors person, and her personal list includes hiking, kayaking, skiing, and camping. On her professional list, she identified that she enjoys managing trade shows and other customer-focused events. Linda put managing trade shows for a sporting goods or outdoor gear manufacturer on her potential career avenues list. To locate these types of companies, Linda is looking at a number of associations that focus on the sporting goods industry. She's exploring Web sites such as www.trailspace.com/gear/brands that provide an alphabetical list of outdoor gear manufacturers and the Sporting Goods Manufacturers Association's Web site at www.sgma.com.

Many of the companies Linda is targeting are headquartered in different areas than she currently resides. In addition to possibly relocating, Linda may need to consider other factors. She'll want to run through her personal Preference List before she begins putting this job option on her Personal Marketing Plan.

In Chapter Two, you'll begin evaluating your list of preferences. Even if a job allows you the opportunity to travel all over the world or plan the most amazing conferences or events, your preferences have a tremendous influence on your overall sense of satisfaction; in some cases, they can make or break a job.

EXAMPLE: SUSAN BRIGHT'S

PERSONAL AND PROFESSIONAL WISH LIST

View 1: Interests Not Ranked

PERSONAL INTERESTS	RANK/ NTR	PROFESSIONAL INTERESTS	RANK/ NTR
Playing golf		Coordinating trade shows on an international level	
Hiking		Designing registration Web sites for internal/ external clients	
Gardening		Putting together golf tournaments	
Knitting		Planning incentive programs	
Cooking and baking		Managing a meeting planning department	
Volunteering with local Habitat for Humanity chapter		Being involved in the marketing strategy for meetings and events	
Volunteering at child's school		Working closely with senior management on strategic goals	
Supporting Nature Conservancy		Creating databases to manage program information	

EXAMPLE: SUSAN BRIGHT'S

PERSONAL AND PROFESSIONAL WISH LIST

View 2: Interests Ranked

PERSONAL INTERESTS	RANK/ NTR	PROFESSIONAL INTERESTS	RANK/ NTR
Playing golf	1	Coordinating trade shows on an international level	5
Hiking	7	Designing registration Web sites for internal/ external clients	6
Gardening	4	Putting together golf tournaments	1
Knitting	5	Planning incentive programs	2
Baking	6	Managing a meeting planning department	8
Volunteering with local Habitat for Humanity chapter	2	Being involved in the marketing strategy for meetings and events	4
Volunteering at child's school	3	Working closely with senior management on strategic goals	3
Supporting Nature Conservancy	8	Creating databases to manage program information	7

EXAMPLE: SUSAN BRIGHT'S

PERSONAL AND PROFESSIONAL WISH LIST

View 3: Need to Research (NTR)

PERSONAL INTERESTS	RANK/ NTR	PROFESSIONAL INTERESTS	RANK/ NTR
Playing golf		Coordinating trade shows on an international level	
Hiking		Designing registration Web sites for internal/ external clients	NTR
Gardening		Putting together golf tournaments	
Knitting		Planning incentive programs	
Cooking and baking		Managing a meeting planning department	
Volunteering with local Habitat for Humanity chapter		Being involved in the marketing strategy for meetings and events	NTR
Volunteering at child's school		Working closely with senior management on strategic goals	
Supporting Nature Conservancy		Creating databases to manage program information	

Chapter Two

PERSONAL PREFERENCES THAT IMPACT CAREER CHOICES

Besides the salary and responsibilities a new position offers, there are a number of other factors to take into consideration before accepting a job. For example, we all have personal preferences about issues that impact us on the job. Some of these issues include where you prefer working (locally, regionally, globally), how far or how much time you'd be willing to spend commuting to a job, your preferred work environment (cubicle, separate office, or open space), and the type of management style under which you flourish.

Everyone's list of preferences looks different because these types of issues may be more or less important to people. The level of importance each item plays in our lives may change over time, so be sure to reassess your Preference List as you progress with your career. In addition to reassessing your list before you begin a new job search, I'd also recommend reviewing it at least once every year or two to keep it updated.

Preference List

Although this list includes different factors to take into consideration when you evaluate job opportunities, you may have other items that are important to you that you want to add to your list (see the example on pages 21–24).

1) Location of the Job

Determine if you have specific areas where you prefer to work.

- ✓ Assess your preferences about working in specific cities. Do you prefer working in a major metropolitan city or a smaller, more suburban location? Does your mode of transportation impact this decision?
- ✓ Ask yourself if there are cities, states, or regions of the country you would like to live in or ones you would avoid.
- ✓ Do you have an interest in relocating to another part of the United States or to another country?

2) Commute Tolerance

Unless you're living in a remote part of the country, commute traffic has become a common issue in most cities across the United States. The difference is that everyone has a different amount of time they're willing to be on the road getting to and from work. Some people have less tolerance for commuting, so they may consider only jobs that require thirty minutes or less of driving time. Other people are willing to travel a greater distance for a job; they have no problem driving ninety minutes or more to get to their job each day. Once you figure out your commute zone, you can create a target list of companies within that area.

For some people, a critical issue is *how* they get to work. Many individuals who live in a major metropolitan city no longer own a vehicle so public transportation is the only way they can get to work. People who live in outlying suburbs from major metropolitan areas may have train systems, but it may not be easy to use them. It may be difficult to find parking close to the train station; parking might be expensive to use on a daily basis; trains may not run enough hours in the evening to accommodate working late; or the station closest to the office may not be in an area that's safe once it's dark outside.

A major consideration for those who drive to work is the cost of gasoline. This was especially true when the price of gas exceeded $4 a gallon. At that price, it could cost over $1,800 a year just for gas if a person's job was twenty-five miles away. That's not factoring in additional travel costs such as bridge tolls and parking. These types of increased costs may make you consider options closer to home.

To help offset these costs, many companies and organizations offer reimbursement for commuting costs as a benefit to their employees. A trade association in New York offers their employees vouchers for public transportation. In San Francisco, a financial services company provides $200 per month to employees who have to drive to work to help offset the cost of parking downtown.

The dilemma for job seekers occurs when they find a great job opportunity but the daily commute is longer than they would prefer. Oftentimes the lengthy commute begins to take its toll and the person ends up leaving the job. That's why it's critical to assess whether the value of the job will outweigh the stress and amount of personal time lost due to the lengthy commute.

There are a couple of reasons to avoid this type of situation:

✓ Staying in jobs for short periods does not look good on a resume.
✓ Poor decisions like this make future employers question your ability to assess situations; it also makes them wonder if you would do the same thing to them.

3) Work Setting

I always ask job seekers what type of work setting they prefer. The three most common types of office settings used these days include: cubicle environment, separate offices, and an open office space (also referred to as an "open landscape"). The open office is a phenomenon that companies such as Intel, Cisco, and Google have begun embracing because it fosters more productivity and interaction among team members. It also reduces the cost of building and maintaining work environments such as cubicles.

Telecommuting and Virtual Offices

Two work environments currently used allow employees to work outside the office—telecommuting and virtual offices. Given the fact that a significant amount of work employees do today is on computers, it's surprising that more companies still do not offer the option to work from a remote location. In a study done by the Urban Land Institute in 2007, only 21 percent of companies with one hundred or more employees said they offer telecommuting, while 45 percent said they offer flextime schedules.

The Urban Land Institute's study also asked companies whether they would alter their policies regarding telecommuting given the rising cost of gasoline. Based on this information, 29 percent of the companies responding said they planned to allow employees to telecommute every day, 16 percent said they would allow telecommuting one or two days a week, and 17 percent said they would consider allowing telecommuting if enough employees requested it.

Companies that embrace telecommuting find that employees who telecommute are 10 to 15 percent more productive than when they work in an office on a daily basis. With commuting costs rising, it's likely that the percentage of companies offering telecommuting will increase dramatically.

In 2007 Runzheimer International performed a *Total Employee Mobility Benchmarking Study* based on leading U.S. and Canadian corporations. Runzheimer defined a "virtual office employee" as anyone who spends at least 60 percent of business hours away from the traditional office setting. The results showed that almost one-third (31 percent) of the respondents expected to increase their spending on virtual office programs, and that these same companies anticipated a 41 percent increase in the number of employees that would shift to a virtual office setting.

Companies such as American Express and PricewaterhouseCoopers (PwC) have been very successful with creating virtual meetings departments. PwC is so committed to the concept of virtual meetings that they have a virtual meeting manager who oversees a department of virtual meeting planners responsible for planning virtual meetings for PwC employees worldwide.

If there's a job that you're interested in that's farther than you'd care to commute on a daily basis, be sure to investigate whether the company or organization has a policy about telecommuting or supports a virtual office. As these studies indicate, an increasing number of employers are looking at shifting in these directions.

4) Size of the Company

Think about the company or organization where you most enjoyed working. Was it small, medium, or large in terms of the total number of employees? Some individuals are most comfortable working where there are fewer employees (fewer than ten) because they are able to get involved in more areas of the planning process. Others prefer working in a large company where roles and responsibilities are more structured and where it's necessary to interface with a variety of internal departments for marketing and communications, accounting, etc.

If you're considering applying for a job with a smaller or larger company or organization than you've had experience working in, contact business associates who work in one of a similar size. You should develop a list of questions about things that are of concern to you. These are a few things you might want to ask them: How are decisions made within the meetings department and within the company/organization as a whole? Do meeting planners work independently or within a team process? How is the meetings department viewed within the company/organization—are they tactical implementers or strategic partners?

5) Type of Company or Organization

One of the wonderful things about being a meeting planner is that there are so many industries and types of organizations that require your services. Take the high-tech industry for example. The obvious companies to target are the primary hardware and software manufacturers—companies such as Hewlett Packard, Cisco Systems, Dell, Adobe, Apple Computers, and Microsoft. What people sometimes forget to look at are the companies that manufacture the parts and programs that support the high-tech industry, such as Intel, AMD, etc.

In addition to companies, trade associations produce conferences and trade shows that support the high-tech industry. Some, such as Semiconductor Equipment and Materials International (SEMI) serve a global audience, while others, such as the Hawaii Technology Trade Association (HTTA), deal with a more regionally focused membership. The Consumer Electronics Association produces one of the largest shows geared toward the high-tech industry—the Consumer Electronics Show held each year in Las Vegas. These types of trade associations would be good to put on your target list if the personal side of your Wish List includes an interest in information technology, and the professional side shows that you enjoy planning association meetings and trade shows.

This same approach works with anything you're interested in pursuing. Let's say you wanted to explore working in the apparel industry. There are a myriad of avenues to explore, such as working for an apparel or footwear designer, a fashion magazine, or a national chain of clothing or shoe stores. As with the high-tech industry, there are numerous trade associations that support each of these fashion-related industries.

Special Knowledge Required

It's important to keep in mind that some industries may require knowledge about specific restrictions and regulations they have about planning meetings. Take the pharmaceutical industry. Based on a compliance program initiated by the U.S. Office of the Inspector General in 2003, the Pharmaceutical Research and Manufacturers of America released a detailed code of ethics for pharmaceutical companies. The purpose was to reverse the abuses of pharmaceutical companies, which included asking physicians to use their products in exchange for lavish trips and gifts. Now referred to as PhRMA codes, meeting planners must understand and comply with restrictions about who can attend meetings and the type of location or property considered appropriate for a meeting. As of 2009, pharmaceutical companies will not be allowed to distribute "non-educational" items to health care providers and their staff, such as pens, coffee mugs, tote bags and any other promotional items with the pharmaceutical company's logo. This changes what a pharmaceutical company can do at trade shows. These changes can and will impact the relationship meeting planners have with suppliers to the pharmaceutical industry, such as specialty gift companies.

6) Work Environment

There's no doubt that the type of manager you work with can and will affect your effectiveness in a department. The situation probably wouldn't work if you prefer operating in a more independent fashion, yet your supervisor is very controlling and requires you to report in to her or him on a regular basis. The same is true if you prefer having direct interaction with your supervisor, and the supervisor has a more hands-off approach with her or his staff. You may become resentful if your manager isn't available to provide supervision and support. This happens frequently when the manager of a meetings department tries to balance supervising a team of planners while being directly responsible for managing a number of meetings and events.

Some people operate best in a team environment, some when they can manage all aspects of a program on their own, while others like a balance of the two situations. This is an important issue that hiring managers frequently ask about during interviews. At a trade association in California, the hiring manager asks each candidate to "describe the amount of structure, direction, and feedback they need to excel." She also asks each candidate to describe a supervisor or boss that they liked working with and didn't like working with, and why.

Dress Code – Casual or Business Attire

People oftentimes forget to ask if a company or organization has a specific dress code. The dot-com era brought about a number of changes for employees; one change was that casual attire became an acceptable way to dress for work. Eventually, casual dress spread to other areas of the business sector, including the financial and insurance industries.

Unfortunately, some employees took casual too far and as a result, many companies are shifting back to a more formal dress code. One of the factors influencing the type of dress code a company or organization establishes is the level of interaction employees have with customers and its members.

An association based in New York City has a formal dress code for employees because their members include owners and management companies in the real estate industry. Candidates receive information about wearing business attire when they interview for positions (for women that means suits with skirts); individuals who appear in casual attire tend to receive less than favorable consideration as candidates.

The same holds true for employers who have a more relaxed dress code. It might make the hiring manager at one of these companies or organizations uncomfortable if you arrived in a business suit. Whether the employer allows a more casual style or requires business suits, make sure that it matches with the way you like to dress for work.

7) Amount of Travel Managing Programs

A lot of people outside of the meetings industry have the impression that getting to travel to different places must be a great perk of the job. That is, until you tell them about the long hours you work during a program and the fact that you have very limited time—or in most cases, none at all—to explore the destination where the program happens.

Although travel is required for a majority of meeting planners, it's important to know how much you're comfortable doing as part of the job. It's not a function of age—it has more to do with the other priorities in your life. I spoke to a young woman who had been planning meetings for less than five years and on average, she was traveling more than 50 percent of the time each month. In the beginning, she enjoyed traveling to places she hadn't been to before. Things began to shift when she realized that her job had become the focus of her life. Her family and friends starting leaving messages that they couldn't remember the last time they'd seen her, and her plants kept dying in the apartment because she wasn't there enough to tend to them!

Although this may be a bit of an extreme situation, the point is that you need to assess how much travel you're comfortable doing, whether it's less than 20 percent, 25 percent, 50 percent, or more than that. In many cases, job descriptions will indicate the level of travel required; if it doesn't, it is definitely a question you should be asking during the interview process.

8) Relocating for a Job

Sometimes you have to consider relocating to another area for a job if you want to give a boost to your career. It isn't the easiest decision to make unless you're single, don't own a home, and have no friends or family who live nearby. Once you start sinking roots into an area, it becomes more difficult to cut those ties.

Factors to consider include the cost of living in the new city, job opportunities for your spouse or partner, and school systems and other activities for your children. Chapter Six examines in detail these aspects and others that you'll need to consider if relocation is a consideration.

As you move along in your career AND your life, your priorities will change so be sure to revisit this list before you make your next move.

PREFERENCE LIST

ITEM	VERY IMPORTANT	NOT IMPORTANT	FLEXIBLE: DEPENDS ON JOB
JOB LOCATION: Within a specific city			
Within a specific local region (e.g., San Francisco Bay Area)			
Anywhere in a specific state			
Within a U.S. region (e.g., Pacific Northwest)			
Anywhere in the United States			
Other countries: SPECIFY			
Anywhere globally			
COMMUTE TOLERANCE: Less than 30 minutes each way			
Up to 60 minutes each way			
Up to 90 minutes each way			
Need to determine parking costs			

ITEM	VERY IMPORTANT	NOT IMPORTANT	FLEXIBLE: DEPENDS ON JOB
Must be accessible by public transportation			
Employer pays for or subsidizes cost of transportation			
WORK SETTING: Need a separate office			
Work in cubicle setting			
Telecommute (note preferred number of days per week)			
Virtual office setting			
COMPANY SIZE: Fewer than 10 employees			
11–25 employees			
26–50 employees			
51–100 employees			
101–500 employees			
More than 500 employees			

PERSONAL PREFERENCES

ITEM	VERY IMPORTANT	NOT IMPORTANT	FLEXIBLE: DEPENDS ON JOB
TYPE OF EMPLOYER: Corporation			
Association			
Non-profit			
Meeting management company			
Other: DESCRIBE			
WORK ENVIRONMENT: Work autonomously			
Work with a team			
Mix of individual and team process			
WORK STYLE & DRESS: Casual			
Formal			
TYPE OF MANAGER: Direct supervision			
Allows autonomous work			

ITEM	VERY IMPORTANT	NOT IMPORTANT	FLEXIBLE: DEPENDS ON JOB
WORK SCHEDULE: In-house full-time			
Telecommuting			
Flexible schedule			
AMOUNT OF TRAVEL TO MANAGE PROGRAMS:			
25% or less			
26–50%			
More than 50%			
RELOCATION ISSUES: Selling current home			
Cost of buying home in new city			
Having employer pay for all or a portion of the relocation expenses			
Ability for spouse/ partner to find work			

Chapter Three

FORMULATING YOUR PERSONAL MARKETING PLAN

Once you identify a potential career avenue, the next step is to formulate a plan of action so you can make this a reality. Just sending out your resume to jobs posted on career boards and hoping you get a response is a very passive approach. Because there are so many highly qualified meeting professionals out there, you need to figure out how to make yourself stand out in the crowd. You need to identify what makes you unique and different. Once you do, you'll use this information to create a Personal Marketing Plan that identifies your skills and abilities and the best way for you to sell them to prospective employers.

Step One: Establish Your Unique Selling Propositions

When a company considers how to market a product or service, it focuses on the item's unique selling proposition (USP). It may be that the item or service costs less, works more efficiently, or lasts longer. This is what differentiates the company's product or service from others in the marketplace.

Instead of marketing a gadget or a service, think of this from the perspective that **you** are the product. Your Personal Marketing Plan should focus on your USPs—those skills and abilities that make you unique and a better candidate than any other applicant in the job market.

Think about the skills and abilities you already have that you included on your Wish List. Consider how a company or organization could benefit from your USPs.

Step Two: Identifying Your Personal Brand

A key element to marketing is to establish a brand for a product or service—an image that allows people to easily identify this product or service from the competition. Companies and organizations spend thousands of dollars to create and maintain their brands. Think of your favorite soft drink, ice cream, computer, or a well-known organization. Take jeans, for example. A manufacturer creates a brand based on the things that make its jeans different from everyone else's.

Your personal brand includes the skills and abilities you've gained that have become your areas of specialty. What skills and abilities would one of your references identify as areas where you excel if contacted by a prospective employer? Maybe you have become extremely knowledgeable about strategic planning, budget design, or have become an expert in contract negotiations. Think of these as your brand. Your brand also encompasses any specific types of meetings you have expertise managing, such as trade shows, product launches, seminar series, incentive travel programs, annual meetings, or general sessions.

Now think about the types of industries, companies, and organizations that could benefit from your unique selling propositions and your brand. These are the target markets you'll want to focus on in your Personal Marketing Plan.

Step Three: Your Target Contact List

The next step is to develop a list of companies and organizations you believe match with the career goal you established based on your Wish

List. You'll need to do some research to create a list of people to contact. If you belong to any professional associations, their membership directories are a rich source for mining prospects to contact. Another good place to check is the local chamber of commerce directory for businesses in the areas you're targeting. To find out information about a company, I highly recommend checking out Hoovers at www. hoovers.com. Besides providing a company overview, Hoovers offers a competitor summary that includes a list of a company's key competitors, as well as the company's significant developments or products. In addition to the company's headquarters location, Hoovers also lists any subsidiary companies; this may be helpful if a subsidiary is located in an area that is better suited to your search criteria. You'll also find a link to the company's Web site so you can perform a more extensive search.

Your Own Network of Contacts

In addition to identifying specific companies, you'll want to tap into your network of contacts. This list includes former coworkers and supervisors as well as people you've met professionally and in your personal life.

Former coworkers and supervisors are a great resource because they already know about the quality of your work. It's likely these individuals will move on to other jobs as well, so be sure to keep in contact with them on a regular basis. It's especially important to keep in contact with these people if you have them listed as a reference. Update them about your career strategy and be sure to point out the skills and abilities they would have experienced when working with you that relate to your new focus and direction.

Another group of contacts that people oftentimes forget about are the ones they've met professionally and in their personal life. Think about all of the people you've met at professional association meetings and at other industry-related events. Similar to the people you've met through your jobs, these people are valuable sources, especially if you've been involved with them on committees through your professional associations.

Consider contacting people you met through college or any advanced training or certification programs (i.e., programs for Certified Meeting Professionals, Certified Meeting Managers, Certified Trade Show Managers, etc.). Consider as well the people you've met through your volunteer involvement, through any religious or cultural groups you belong to, and people you've met through your children's outside activities, such as soccer, swim team, or band.

All of these people have networks of individuals they know who may bring you closer to achieving your career goal. This process is oftentimes referred to as "six degrees of separation." This is the theory that we are one step away from knowing someone and two steps away from the person he or she knows, which means that we are all just six steps away from knowing every person on Earth.

This is the premise employed by social networking sites such as Facebook, LinkedIn, and Ning. By connecting with one individual you know, you can tap into their connections to help expand your own network. These sites contain subgroups that you can join such as college alumni, people who worked for a particular company, those interested in a specific cause or personal interest. For example, on Ning you can join a group called the Meeting Planners and Hoteliers Network or, if you love playing golf, there's a Golf's World Network. On LinkedIn, you can join a group of Certified Meeting Professionals (CMPs). One word of caution: human resource managers use these same websites to identify prospective candidates, so be sure not to put anything in your profile that you wouldn't want your current employer to read.

Whether you use an online source or make contact in a more direct manner, the key is to enlist the services of as many people as possible who can assist you with reaching your career goal.

Step Four: Create Your Personal Marketing Plan

Your Personal Marketing Plan should be **specific, realistic, flexible, and have measurable goals.** It needs to include specific action items that you want to complete. These items need to be measureable so that you can determine how well you achieved them. Be realistic about what you can achieve and how and when you can achieve these goals. Most likely, you're doing this while you're working full-time, so make certain that you allow yourself some flexibility to adjust completion dates because work may get in the way of your job search.

If you search from work, be careful which Web sites you visit because employers can see where you're going on the Internet. If you send your resume from work, be sure to use your personal email address because employers can open up your company email. In one case, a third-party meeting management company found out that a junior meeting planner had applied for a job with one of their clients. Not only had the individual kept her resume on her computer at work, she also kept a folder with her email communications with the client. Avoid having this type of electronic "paper trail" that your employer can find. Although it's more restrictive, it's best to maintain your job search away from work.

To help guide you through this process, write out a simple mission statement about your career goal. A personal mission statement identifies your values and the direction you want to go with your career. Goals state the achievements you must accomplish to attain your personal mission statement. (For more specifics on developing a personal mission statement, I recommend checking Quintessential Careers Web site at www.quintcareers.com/creating_personal_mission_statements.html)

Example of a Mission Statement:

To move into a senior management position that oversees trade shows for a company related to the aviation industry.

Below your mission statement, list the target markets you've identified based on your unique selling propositions and your brand. (See the sample Personal Marketing Plan Worksheet on page 33.)

Your Plan of Action identifies the steps you want to take to achieve your mission statement. Place items on a time line, identifying how long you think it will take to achieve each of them. Establish a separate column for an anticipated completion date, the actual completion date, and a comment field so that you can make notations about how long it took to complete this action item, and what happened if you had delays. Maybe you had to manage an unexpected project at work and it required you to stop working on your action items for a couple of weeks. Don't get discouraged if it takes longer than you anticipated to achieve your career goal; the comment field will help remind you why there were gaps along the way.

An important element of your Plan of Action is a target completion date. This date will help keep you focused on your ultimate goal—the date you'd like to be in your new job. As you begin completing tasks in your Personal Marketing Plan, you may need to revise your target date if you find that your efforts move you in a new direction with your career goal.

Review and Reassess Your Plan

Companies and organizations have annual board retreats to review and reassess their mission statements and strategic goals. Whether you anticipate achieving your career goal in three months or three years, be sure to reassess your Personal Marketing Plan periodically to make sure that it still matches with your personal priorities and your professional goals.

Opportunities can appear unexpectedly from places different than you may envision. I have a quote from Helen Keller hanging in my office to remind me about this perspective. She once said, "When one door of happiness closes, another opens; but often we look so long at the closed door that we do not see the one which has opened for us." Before you decline an unexpected opportunity, explore whether it allows you to make your Wish List come true. Although it looks different than you thought it would, this alternative job may move you closer to or actually put you in the position you're seeking.

The key is to use your career strategy as a guide to help you determine whether a job opportunity is a good fit. Does it take you in the direction you're aiming with your personal priorities and professional goals?

While you're developing a Personal Marketing Plan, you'll need to focus on your resume. Whether you're creating your first resume or doing some updating, **most** job seekers find this is the most difficult task because they're uncertain how much information to include about their background and experience. Typically, a resume ends up either saying too much or too little about a person's abilities. With increased competition for jobs, it's important for your resume to stand out from all others. Your resume must convince the meeting manager or the manager in human resources that you're a candidate he or she *must* interview.

Personal Marketing Plan Worksheet

My mission statement: _____

_____

Target Completion Date (getting my new job): _____

My target contact list (include specific markets and industries):

1. _____ 5. _____
2. _____ 6. _____
3. _____ 7. _____
4. _____ 8. _____

Action Plan:

The MeetingConnection

© 1/08 The MeetingConnection

33

Chapter Four

BUILD A RESUME THAT BEST REFLECTS YOUR ACCOMPLISHMENTS AND ACHIEVEMENTS

One of the misconceptions people have about putting together a resume is that it needs to include details about everything they did in every job they've ever held. Your resume shouldn't be a complete recounting of your past work experience. Instead, you want it to highlight the skills, abilities, and accomplishments that support the direction you want to go with your career. You want your resume to reflect the stepping-stones in your work experience that relate to your career goal. Whether you state an objective or not, your resume provides the reader with a sense as to what you want to achieve.

Another misconception is that resumes are just a formality. Some people believe that it's not necessary to include detailed information in the resume because they'll provide it when they interview for the job. That approach might have worked when employers received resumes in the mail and fewer of them than they do today. Hiring managers had the time to read every resume thoroughly. If one didn't provide enough detailed information but the hiring manager saw something of interest in a candidate's background, the manager would be willing to invite the individual in for an interview to determine the candidate's suitability.

Many people also think that the cover letter is the only place where they're supposed to provide information about their background and experience that's relevant to the posted position. If you submit your resume electronically (see details about this process in Chapter Five), there's a good chance that your cover letter may not stay attached to your resume. That wouldn't bode well for your resume if it doesn't stand on its own highlighting your qualifications.

Once companies began posting job openings on the Internet, the situation changed dramatically. Now, approximately 85 percent of Fortune 500 companies post jobs on their Web sites and require electronic submission of resumes. In a study done by the Equal Employment Opportunity Commission (EEOC) in 2004, companies that posted their jobs on the Internet received 2.3 times more resumes than they had in the past. For some employers, this could mean receiving one hundred to one thousand resumes instead of fifty to four hundred resumes.

In a study done by Booz Allen Hamilton, a New York consulting company, 51 percent of all positions filled occurred because the individual applied via the Internet. Twenty-one percent of those placements came because candidates applied through a corporation's Web site, while another 21 percent applied through an online job board.

With an increased volume in the number of resumes received, many employers now use an applicant tracking system so they can place all the resumes they receive in a database and then perform keyword searches to help them identify qualified candidates. (Look for more on this in Chapter Five.)

Your Resume is Your Marketing Piece

Given the increased competition online, you need to find a way to make your resume stand out from such a crowded field of candidates. Instead of thinking of your resume as just a record of your work history, think of it as your marketing brochure. As with any marketing material, the goal is to "sell" the buyer on the fact that what's being marketed is the best one to purchase.

In this case, a prospective employer is the buyer who reads your marketing piece—your resume—to determine if he or she wants to acquire your product (your skills, abilities, and accomplishments). Receiving an invitation for an interview depends on how successful you are with your marketing efforts (see the diagram on page 38).

The **_PRODUCT_** is **_YOU_** - Your Skills and Abilities. You want to **_SELL_** this PRODUCT to the BUYER

The Prospective Employer is the **_BUYER_**

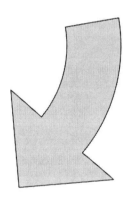

Your **_RESUME_** is the **_MARKETING PIECE_** that SELLS the BUYER on your PRODUCT

You want to incorporate the same unique selling propositions (USPs) and brand in your resume that you identified when you created your Personal Marketing Plan. You want your resume to answer two questions:

1) What makes you a better applicant than any other candidate?
2) What skills and abilities do you offer that will benefit the company or organization where you're applying?

Your resume needs to highlight specific accomplishments and achievements and state them in a tangible and quantifiable manner.

Example: Marsha's responsibilities have included managing exhibitors and sponsors for her association. In the original version of her initial resume, Marsha stated that she, *"Grew Sponsor/Vendor Program 25 percent; established new levels of sponsorship to meet identified market needs."* The problem with this statement is that it lacks specifics about the 25 percent increase and the new levels of sponsorship Marsha established.

What Marsha needs to do is incorporate detailed information about the amount of sponsorship and exhibitor revenue generated as well as specific examples of the new levels created for sponsorship. An alternative would be for her to break this up into two statements:

Sponsorship revenue increased in 2007 by 25 percent to $80,000 and exhibitor revenue by 28 percent to $125,000.

Established a new sponsorship program that meets marketing needs identified by sponsors; sponsorship areas include a speaker appreciation cocktail party, production of the technical digest on a CD-ROM, and a student scholarship.

Avoid Generalities

When meeting planners write that they have "extensive experience planning meetings and events," there is a presumption that whoever reads their resume interprets **meetings and events** in the same way. The assumption is that the reader can read between the lines to know exactly what types of meetings the job seeker managed.

The truth is that there are many ways to interpret the meaning of **meetings and events.** The Convention Industry Council (CIC) is keenly aware of that and as a result, developed an Industry Glossary that contains almost four thousand terms, acronyms, and abbreviations.

The CIC's definition of a **meeting** is: "An event where the primary activity of the attendees is to attend educational sessions, participate in meetings/discussions, socialize, or attend other organized events. There is no exhibit component to this event." The glossary goes on to describe an **event** as, "An organized occasion such as a meeting, convention, exhibition, special event, gala dinner, etc. An event is often composed of several different yet related functions." The glossary identifies more specifically a **corporate meeting** as a "Gathering of employees or representatives of a commercial organization. Usually, attendance is required and travel, room, and most meal expenses are paid for by the organization."

Although these terms help provide a level of agreement as to what or who is involved in a meeting or event, there is another level of detail that a hiring manager is seeking. They want specifics about the types of meetings and events a planner has managed, such as sales meetings, distributor or reseller meetings, Webinars, multiday seminars, training meetings, incentive programs, and employee recognition events. For association meeting planners, hiring managers are looking for specifics about the types of seminars, forums, annual meetings, board of director meetings, and exhibitions the meeting planner has managed.

That's why it's important to avoid using generalized statements when you describe your USPs. For example, Trisha has extensive experience creating Web sites and databases for her association clients, yet her resume didn't clearly communicate her experience level in either of these areas. In the original version of her resume, she simply said, *"Created a Web site for an association."* Providing the reader with more details facilitates a better understanding of the scope of Trisha's capabilities. This statement now reads:

Using computer expertise, created a new Web site for the association that offers members online options to register for educational events online and renew membership.

Be sure to provide specifics about the number and types of attendees, the number of days for the meeting or event, the frequency of the program(s), and the location of the meetings. One way to restate this is, *"Managed meetings with 150–1,500 attendees with programs ranging in length from one to five days."* Another example is, *"Managed up to twenty-four two- to three–day continuing education seminars for dental support staff. Handled registration, confirmed twenty to twenty-five exhibitors for tabletop trade shows, arranged all meal functions, meeting space logistics, and worked with speakers on travel arrangements and presentations."*

If you have experience handling meetings on an international level, be sure to note some of the countries where you managed them. An example of this is, *"Managed twenty-five four-day meetings each year in international locations such as China, Turkey, Spain, and Brazil. Approximately 125 people from senior management attended from each region."*

Make certain to provide details about the scope of your responsibilities. Let's say some of your accomplishments fall in the realm of financial management. Although it might sound impressive that you managed a $15 million meeting management budget, prospective employers also want to know about the types of meetings and events that budget encompassed. To include specifics about the per-program budgets within a range, you might say, *"Managed a $15 million meeting management budget that included per-program budgets ranging in size from $15,000–$1.5 million (President's Circle incentive)."* If one of your USPs is your ability to reduce costs, note tangible examples, such as: *"reduced program expenses by 15 percent on an annual basis"* or *"decreased program expenses by $10,000 per year."*

Be sure to highlight your brand—the skills and experience you've gained to form your area(s) of specialty. If you are seeking a position that utilizes your strategic skills, then make sure your resume emphasizes this area rather than your logistics or operations experience.

One young meeting planner was puzzled why she continually ended up in positions where she was responsible for designing invitations for her company's parties and special events. The reason was that every job on her resume included a bullet that stated her experience in this area. She created a brand for herself that she didn't really want!

Designing Your Resume

The design and layout of a marketing piece influence how people receive the information. Eyes tend to gravitate from the top to the bottom when you're reading a document. That's why it's important to prioritize information about each job so that the most relevant items appear first.

On average, hiring managers spend anywhere from ten to twenty seconds initially reading a resume. Given this short time frame, it is important that you do everything to help ensure that the reader gets all the way through your resume. By placing your information in a bulleted format instead of in paragraphs, you help the reader so that he or she can quickly view all of your accomplishments.

Use clear and concise wording when describing your experience, skills, and background. If a company is looking for someone who has experience planning multicity seminars and product launches, it would be hard to tell that you have that experience if your resume just says, *"Experience coordinating a wide range of meetings and events."* Instead, change this to read, *"Experience coordinating a wide range of meetings and events such as annual user conferences, multicity trainings, sales meetings, and annual sales incentive trips."*

Paragraph or Bullet Format

Given the short amount of time that human resources managers and hiring managers spend initially reviewing a resume, it's important to avoid anything that will slow down the process. Paragraphs tend to take more time to read, so avoid using this format as much as possible. Highlighting specific accomplishments in bulleted descriptions helps the reader to scan more effectively through the whole resume. Think of it as if you're giving descriptive sound bites to the reader. We tend to read information on a page from top to bottom, so remember to place the accomplishments you most want read for each job at the top of the bulleted items.

Information to Include or to Exclude

As your primary marketing piece, you want to keep the reader's focus by highlighting those areas of your past jobs that you enjoyed, have expertise in, and want to expand upon. Make sure not to clutter your resume with information that will distract the reader or shift his or her focus from your brand.

The general rule of thumb is to show no more than ten to twelve years of experience on a resume. If there is a job before that time that you believe is relevant, there are a number of ways to include this information.

One option is to add a section called "Previous Experience," under which you simply list the name of the company, your title, city, state, and dates of employment. Another option is to create an addendum for your resume where you highlight specific meetings and events. Describe each meeting or event in a brief paragraph and include information about your specific responsibilities. (See Chapter Seven for more information about creating an addendum.)

Comparable Experience

Realtors frequently look for comparables when they are trying to determine a sales price to list or buy a home. Comparables are homes in the neighborhood with a similar amount of square footage, number of rooms, and amenities. With jobs, hiring managers are seeking candidates who have comparable experience that matches with the size and types of programs the company or organization offers. The key for candidates is to provide as many details as possible so the hiring manager clearly sees that they have the comparable skills needed for the job.

Employers like to see specific references to your accomplishments, so be sure to quantify your achievements such as decreasing costs, increasing revenue, or improving attendance. An example of this would be, *"Increased exhibitor participation by 25 percent up to two hundred booths in one year by including more conference-related activities in the exhibit hall."* If you want to show your ability to reduce costs, you might say, *"Reduced the operating budget by 15 percent, saving the company over $75,000 on an annual basis."*

Review your resume to make certain that you are including the following information:

✓ Size of the Programs: This information helps prospective employers know if you have experience working with programs of a size similar to the ones their departments handle. Let them know this information by stating a range of the size of meetings (twenty-five to twenty-five hundred participants), a maximum number (up to twenty-five hundred participants), or an average program size (average of five hundred attendees).

✓ Frequency of the Programs: This information allows employers to determine whether you have experience handling a similar volume of meetings and events. If you're applying for a job in a meetings department that produces one hundred seminars every quarter and you've handled only five to ten seminars per year, the hiring manager may not see you as a good fit. You want to identify the number of programs you manage on a monthly and/or annual basis, i.e., *"in charge of approximately five meetings per month, ranging in size from twenty-five to five hundred participants"* or *"approximately thirty-five meetings and events per year with the largest being the annual meeting with up to three thousand attendees."*

✓ Types of Programs: Hiring managers want to know if you have planned meetings and events similar to the ones their department typically handles. Be sure to indicate if you have planned sales meetings, seminars, trainings, user conferences, annual conferences, board of directors, multicity programs, product launches, incentive trips, or trade shows.

✓ Location of the Meetings: Provide more details than just "plan domestic and international meetings." Indicate the number of cities where you have planned meetings domestically, such as *"Arranged seminars in over 250 cities nationwide on an annual basis."* When it comes to international destinations, be as specific as possible. It's not enough to say, *"managed programs in over twenty-five countries."* Include information about specific cities and countries, such as *"Managed programs in over twenty-five countries, including Italy, France, Germany, Singapore, Australia, Brazil, and Mexico."*

By visiting corporate or association Web sites, you can find out where they hold their meetings or the cities where they attend trade shows. The more information you provide that clearly indicates your related experience, the easier it is for a hiring manager to assess whether you have the potential to fit into a department.

If you're looking at switching from being an association planner to working on the corporate side, or if you're a supplier looking to become a planner, you need to focus on rewording your resume so that it communicates your skills and experience from this new direction.

Original Text:

Responsible for the execution of educational conferences, trade shows and networking events that support bioanalytical, pharmaceutical, and separation scientists in the biotechnology and pharmaceutical industries.

Revised Text:

Responsible for the execution of seven annual conferences and four networking dinners held in domestic and international locations for members in the biotechnology and pharmaceutical industries. Meetings range in size from 100-500 attendees and include up to fifty exhibitors per meeting.

Limited or No Experience

A frequent problem for job seekers is how to represent positions where meeting planning responsibilities were either a small or non-existent portion of the position. You can't eliminate these jobs from your resume because employers don't like to see gaps in the chronology of someone's work history.

If that's the case, then how do you address unrelated jobs on your resume? What you want to do is look at these jobs to determine whether any of the responsibilities relate to the meeting planning process. Maybe a job entailed negotiating contracts with vendors or managing budgets. Maybe you had a job where you had to select sites for other events. For example, I've worked with several people in the film industry whose jobs entailed *scouting for locations*. In the meetings industry this is described as *doing a site search*. By using the meetings industry language, you ensure that the reader clearly understands that the person has relevant experience.

If you're unable to find anything that relates to the planning process, then limit the description about this job to a couple of one-line bullets. It's best to minimize the focus on these non-meeting planning jobs.

A functional resume is another way to deal with this issue. This resume format highlights people's job experiences by placing them under specific categories of work, such as meeting management, marketing, computer skills, etc. Positions appear chronologically at the bottom of the resume, as follows:

Job History

Event Manager, Boyler and Associates, Norfolk, VA   *1990–1993*
Assistant Marketing Manager, Saddlemakers, Inc., Dallas, TX   *1989–1990*

A note about functional resumes: Employers aren't always comfortable with a functional resume because they can't clearly distinguish whether the experience relates to one job or multiple jobs, or when the individual did the work. It could be something the person did ten years ago and hasn't had any recent experience dealing with. Another concern for employers is that functional resumes make it difficult to determine if there are gaps in a person's work history. Even if you're the most qualified person for the job, many employers won't allocate the time needed to assess a candidate if they're presented with a functional resume.

Age-Related Information

More and more people are selecting meeting planning as a career. The interest is from people just graduating from college as well as individuals looking to make a change in their career. By law, prospective employers cannot ask questions about a candidate's age, nor can they discriminate against an individual because of age. The truth is that age can be a factor, especially if the manager is younger than his or her staff; unfortunately, some people are uncomfortable managing older staff members who may have more experience than they.

It's best to err on the side of caution and eliminate any specific reference to your age in your resume. A couple of ways that people unknowingly include this information is when they make statements such as "More than twenty years' experience working in a corporate environment" or they include the date they graduated from college. The date you graduated from college can backfire on you whether you're a recent graduate or you graduated fifteen to twenty years ago. An employer performing a thorough background check can verify this information, so just note your degree, your major, and the name of the college or university you attended.

What you don't want to do is note if you attended only a couple of years of college but never completed a degree. It gives the impression that you don't follow through with things, and you don't want a prospective employer to get that kind of impression. Even if a job posting states that a college degree is required, it's better not to include partially completed work. I've spoken to hiring managers over the years about this particular issue, and overwhelmingly they've told me that they'll consider a candidate if his or her experience more than satisfies the stated job requirements. The lack of a college degree may come up later if you're being considered for a management level position, in which case you may need to go back and complete your undergraduate degree.

Senior Level or Management Positions

The exception to indicating your age is if you are applying for a senior level or management position. Here, it is important to include the length of time you've been involved in the meeting planning industry because the employer is looking for a certain level of knowledge and expertise in the field.

Candidates seeking senior level positions often wonder if they should eliminate any reference to their logistical experience and focus only on their strategic abilities. Although the position may not require the individual to handle the logistics directly, it is still important to indicate one's knowledge of the basic planning components—site selection, contract negotiations, on-site management—as well as computer skills. The key is to emphasize the strategic aspects of your experience, so put these accomplishments first and the logistical experience at the bottom section of that particular job.

Multiple Positions Held

How do you present having held multiple positions at the same company? People frequently make the mistake of showing each position with the name of the company—as if the jobs aren't connected.

Meeting Manager, Boyler and Associates, San Francisco, CA 7/05 – 8/08
Responsible for managing more than 50 meetings per year, including the annual sales meeting, product launches.

Project Manager, Boyler and Associates, San Francisco, CA 3/03 – 7/05
Assisted with coordinating the annual sales meeting for 550 people and the seminar series that included 12 cities, each with 75 to 100 attendees per city.

If the hiring manager is quickly scanning the resume, he or she may see the separate dates of employment and not immediately connect that the positions were with the same company. A red flag for employers is a candidate who's held a series of positions for short time frames; they refer to these types of individuals as "job hoppers." To avoid getting labeled this way, it's best to present your jobs in a more consolidated fashion:

Boyler and Associates, San Francisco, CA   **3/03 – 8/08**
- Meeting Manager (7/05 – 8/08)
Responsible for managing more than 50 meetings per year, including the annual sales meeting, product launches
- Project Manager (3/03 – 7/05)
Assisted with coordinating the annual sales meeting for 550 people and the seminar series that included 12 cities, each with 75 to 100 attendees per city.

Contract or Project-Based Work

Nowadays, it is not surprising to see that an individual has shifted back and forth from full-time positions to contract/project-based assignments. If you completed several assignments during a block of time, group them under one header and then list each client along with details about each project. Some headers commonly used are "Contract Assignments" or "Independent Consulting Assignments":

Independent Consulting Assignments   **1/06 – 2008**
ABC Meeting Management, Houston, TX (2007–2008)
-Managed a high-tech conference for XYZ Corporation that included 1,500 attendees, a 250-booth exhibition and 40 speakers...
Meetings and More, Jacksonville, FL (2006–2007)
-Acted as the Assistant Event Manager for a 25-city launch for HIJ's new software

If you took on a single contract assignment between two periods of full-time work, then make sure to identify that it was just a contract assignment. This will help clarify for the prospective employer that it wasn't a position that you started and left too soon.

Highland Internal Medical, Jacksonville, FL   **2006 – 2007**
Assistant Event Manager (Contract Assignment)
-Coordinated a 25-city launch to introduce HIM's new software product...

In today's job market, it is important to remember that with only twenty seconds of initial viewing time, the resume is a job seeker's major selling tool. The individual with a resume that speaks volumes about his or her background and experience in a clear and concise manner is the one who receives an invitation to interview for the position. Your resume is your foot in the door to new opportunities.

Be descriptive in the most succinct way possible

One of the most challenging tasks when designing your resume is to learn how to be as descriptive as possible about your accomplishments and job responsibilities for each position you've held, while doing this in the most succinct manner. Being simultaneously descriptive and concise may sound like a contradiction. It means not being too flowery in the way you describe your experience. Instead of saying, "As the senior planner, in charge of investigating sites and presenting options for consideration for all meetings and events," say, "Responsible for analyzing and selecting sites for all meetings, events, trade shows, and incentive programs."

Confirm Your Attention to Detail

As a meeting planner, you are presenting yourself as someone who pays attention to details. Make sure your resume receives that same level of attention. Always proofread your resume for typos and grammatical errors. Don't rely exclusively on a word processing program's spell-check feature. It's best to have one or two fresh sets of eyes review your resume. Resumes tend to end up in the circular file (the garbage) if they have typos, grammatical errors, or the chronology of employment dates doesn't match.

Storing and Updating Your Resume

Your resume is an ongoing reflection of your career, so update it on a regular basis. By doing this, you'll avoid having to reconstruct details about your major accomplishments long after the meeting or event occurred.

The reason to update your resume on a regular basis is twofold: 1) to ensure that it's stored in a current software version, and 2) to make certain that you always have ready access to your resume. Software upgrades can typically read a few older versions, but there are some instances when formatting is lost or the file is no longer recognized. Even NASA has experienced this problem. They were unable to access all of the information previously stored about the Viking missions to Mars.

Computer hardware and software has changed significantly since these missions occurred in the late 1970s and early 1980s and as a result, newer systems are unable to read some of the critical data they acquired. NASA had to go back to written files to reconstruct some of the information, while other data may be lost forever because the scientists involved are no longer living.

Given the fluid nature of the job market, it's equally important to have ready access to your resume. If you have your resume stored in a file on your work computer, it's likely that you won't be able to retrieve it if you're laid off suddenly. Even if your resume is on your personal computer, be sure to maintain a current backup file in case your computer crashes. Make it a habit to save your resume to a flash drive or storage hard drive. Like NASA, you may not be able to reconstruct the information.

Your resume is *the* document that gets you in the door for that all-important interview, so make sure it represents you in the way you want to be seen as a meeting professional.

Chapter Five

PASSING THE ELECTRONIC SCREENING TEST

Once you have your career strategy in place and you've established your unique selling propositions and personal brand, it's time to make sure that your resume is ready to send out to prospective employers.

There are two things to keep in mind about resumes in today's job market. One has to do with the content in your resume and the other has to do with the way you format your resume. The two go hand in hand. Even the most qualified candidate won't get the job if this type of system can't read his or her resume. The same holds true for a resume that transmits successfully but doesn't include the necessary information to get the hiring manager's attention.

OCR Stands for Optical Character Recognition

There's an important feature about submitting resumes electronically that most people aren't aware of. It has to do with the type of system that companies or organizations use to screen resumes into their database— it's called an applicant tracking system (ATS). When ATS came out in the early 2000, only mid- to large-sized companies or organizations could afford to use it, but more affordable Web-based systems are available now, so even small companies can utilize this feature to help make their search process more efficient. One of the key features of an ATS is optical character recognition (OCR), which is an artificial intelligence that "reads" the text in your resume and extracts information the company is looking for in candidates.

This process is similar to what happens when you search the Internet using keywords, except the big difference here is that if your resume doesn't contain the appropriate keywords the prospective employer is seeking, your resume won't pop up as a potential candidate.

Employers who use applicant tracking systems enter in keywords that relate to the key qualifications and experience they're looking for in candidates. It works in a similar fashion to doing a search on the Internet.

ATS search resumes in a number of different ways. Some search based on the number of keywords or phrases that match with the specified job description or job qualifications and then rank the resumes that contains the most relevant keywords or phrases. Other ATS rank resumes based on the location of the keywords, meaning resumes with keywords that are more toward the top of the page—and therefore more recent work experience—rank higher than resumes where the keywords appear at the bottom of the page.

With some applicant tracking systems, a company can refine the search process by putting more or less weight on skills by noting those that the candidate *must have, can't have, or don't have.* With this system, a company could specify if resumes *must have a CMP designation.* If a candidate applied who met all of the other required qualifications except the CMP designation, his or her resume might end up ranked toward the bottom of the candidate pool—or even worse, it could end up rejected because it didn't match with this job requirement. This same scenario could eliminate a candidate who applied for a junior-level position and the company specified to reject resumes from candidates who have a master's degree or MBA.

As an applicant, you have no way of knowing whether a prospective employer uses an ATS or not. If you want to ensure that your resume receives the appropriate level of consideration, it's important to design your resume so it passes the ATS screening process.

The more keywords and phrases that appear in your resume, the more likely it is for your resume to surface toward the top of the candidate pool. In some cases, these systems allow companies to reject resumes if there aren't enough keywords that match with the job requirements. Some ATS rank resumes based on the number of matching keywords or the proximity of keywords.

Example: A company is looking for someone with experience managing technical training meetings. An individual's resume will rank higher if it says "responsible for managing a wide range of meetings including sales, technical training, and user conferences," instead of "manage meetings and events."

Here's a list of some keywords you might consider including in your resume: "conferences," "seminars," "training meetings," "product launches," "multicity programs," "trade shows," and "incentive programs."

Other applicant tracking systems employ searches based on phrases or a series of related words such as "strategic player," "return on investment," "budget management and analysis, "tradeshow coordination," or "product launches." Use nouns and phrases that describe technical and professional areas of expertise, such as "developed a program to track return on investment."

Avoid using acronyms because the applicant tracking system might not pick them up. This applies to terms such as BEO (write out "banquet event order" instead), industry designations such as Certified Meeting Professional (CMP), Certified Meeting Manager (CMM), or Certified Trade Show Manager (CTSM), and to professional affiliations.

Tips for Designing a Scannable Resume

Here are some of the things that help ensure your resume successfully scans into a company's database.

✓ Optical character recognition is designed to find your contact information in one location on your resume. OCR only knows to find your contact information at the top of the page, so if you've been putting that information on the bottom or all on one line, that might be the reason you haven't been contacted for interviews. Be sure to place it on the top of your resume. Make sure to stack your information so that your mailing address, e-mail address, and contact phone numbers appear on separate lines.

✓ Keep it simple when it comes to font styles. The best ones to use are Arial, Times Roman, Helvetica, or Courier.

✓ When it comes to electronic resumes, keep it simple! Avoid special formatting such as italics or horizontal lines to divide sections of your resume. Eliminate parentheses around area codes when you list your phone numbers, and use dashes instead. Even bold can confuse OCR so keep that to a minimum. (You can always include these special formats in the version you present at your interview.)

✓ It's also best to keep the font size to 11 points or 12 points. Oftentimes, people use 8-point or 9-point fonts so they can fit all of their information on one page. The problem is that OCR has difficulty "reading" fonts that small.

✓ One page versus multiple pages for a resume: In the past, one page was the accepted format for a resume. Now that companies and organizations have the ability to scan resumes into their system, two pages is more the standard for the length of resume accepted by employers.

✓ Be sure to write out professional affiliations and certifications because the applicant tracking software may misinterpret an acronym for something else. If you want to include CMP, for example, make sure it's in parentheses next to Certified Meeting Professional.

✓ Companies and organizations may have specific guidelines about the type of file formats they accept. They may decline resumes sent in a PDF format or they may want resumes converted to a rich text format (RTF).

✓ Don't assume that your cover letter will stay with your resume. When I surveyed HR managers a few years ago for an article, more than 60 percent of them said that they never forward the cover letter to the hiring manager. That's why I emphasize that your resume needs to be your primary marketing piece!

Another important thing to note about passing an ATS screening is that it allows employers to search their database of candidates with a fresh set of "eyes" for each new position they're filling. Because resumes typically remain in a company's database for six to twelve months, it is possible for them to "find" you again if another position opens up and your skills are a better match.

Chapter Six

THE COST OF RELOCATING FOR A JOB

According to the most recent U.S. census data taken in 2007, 16 percent of people moved to another state for work. This is not surprising because job seekers tend to be more willing to relocate when there is a tight job market. They are also more willing to make that decision whether or not the employer pays for relocation expenses.

According to Atlas Van Lines' 41st Annual Corporate Relocation Survey taken in 2008, 52 percent responded that the "lack of qualified people locally" was the primary external factor that caused them to seek candidates outside of their geographic area. In fact, the response more than doubled from 2002 when only 21 percent felt this was a concern. The Atlas Van Lines survey also found that almost three-fourths of the companies surveyed have some kind of formal relocation policy. What's included in those policies can vary tremendously from a flat fee to cover moving costs to assistance with selling a home.

Even if a company or organization states in a job posting that no relocation assistance is available, you may be able to negotiate to have some expenses covered once you receive the final job offer. For that reason, it is important to determine what your relocation needs are when you start your job search. Would you be satisfied if the employer covered only the cost of moving your household furniture and not your car? Do you feel it is important to have one or two scouting trips to the new area covered by the employer? Create a list of the primary expenses you would like the employer to pay for, and include ancillary items that you would be willing to pay for on your own, if necessary.

What You Can Expect

The Atlas survey revealed a significant change in the number of companies that offer full relocation reimbursement packages. In 2007, 55 percent offered full reimbursement of moving expenses to new hires, whereas 86 percent offered the same level of assistance in 1977. In contrast, the number of companies offering partial reimbursement has increased. Forty-three percent of new hires received a partial reimbursement while only 12 percent of companies offered this option thirty years ago. Additionally, 44 percent received a lump sum payment.

Companies that have tiered relocation policies will tend to offer entry-level employees assistance with moving household goods, storage fees for a specific period of time, limited funds to assist with searching for an apartment or home, and a per diem for lodging and meal expenses en route to the new location.

When it is a mid-level manager or senior-level position, the individual may also receive assistance with selling his or her home and purchasing another one in the new location. In many cases, there is a time limit established for selling the old home on your own and then offering a flat rate to have it sold for you. If the individual is a renter, the policy tends to cover the cost of breaking a lease. The employer will also cover the cost of one or two trips to the new area to scout for a new home. The manager or executive might also receive assistance with childcare, and the spouse may get help finding a new job.

A meeting planner from the Seattle area negotiated a relocation package with her new employer that included all of these items, plus quite a few more. Her new employer agreed to a flat fee to cover the following expenses:

✓ Two scouting trips to the San Francisco Bay Area to look for a new apartment
✓ Moving her household goods
✓ Security deposit and first month's rent in her new apartment
✓ Cancellation fees for breaking her lease with the apartment in Seattle
✓ Set-up fees for establishing phone and cable service

In addition to these items, 69 percent of companies offer to move one automobile while only 49 percent will move a second automobile, 52 percent offer assistance renting a storage facility, and 73 percent offer a temporary living allowance toward rent.

In the end, the employer doubled the anticipated expenses to a total of $10,000. According to figures compiled by the Employee Relocation Council (ERC), which is a national association of companies concerned with employee mobility, this meeting planner negotiated very well because they estimate that the cost to relocate a new hire who rents is $16,177. Where the new hire is a homeowner, the ERC's figures indicate that the average cost for relocation is around $55,000.

Employee Agreements Tied to Relocation Expenses

The Seattle meeting planner agreed that if she stayed through the association's annual convention, she would not have to repay any portion of the relocation expenses. If she left before that time, the association would require her to repay a prorated portion of the cost. In the case of another meeting planner, an association offered to provide a flat $5,000 for moving expenses if she agreed to stay in the position for at least one year. They asked her to repay a prorated portion of the expenses if she left before then.

Tax Deductibility of Relocation Expenses

If you have to pay for all or a portion of your relocation expenses, the IRS uses two tests to determine if you qualify for a relocation tax deduction—time and distance. With the time test, you must work full-time for thirty-nine weeks during the first twelve-month period after arriving at the new job. The distance test requires that your new job must be at least fifty miles farther from your old home than your old job location was from your old home.

The IRS allows deduction of expenses such as the cost of packing and shipping your furniture and other household items, the cost of shipping your pets, and the cost of lodging while in transit to your new job. The IRS Publication 521 on moving expenses explains allowed deductions in more detail. You can download this publication from the IRS at www.irs.gov/.

The other thing to keep in mind is that relocation reimbursement is taxable. The best relocation package includes "grossing up"; this means that the total you're provided includes the amount you'll be taxed. For example, if your relocation costs are $5,000 and you are in the 30 percent tax bracket, your out-of-pocket costs would be $1,500. Under a gross-up plan, you would receive $7,142 (reimbursement expenses divided by one, minus the tax rate) and pay $2,142 in taxes. It's important to remember that this is actually the employer's money and not yours.

The Cost of Interviewing

Unless you are in a senior-level or executive position, it is unlikely these days that the prospective employer will pay to fly you out for an interview. A meeting planner, who had been living away from her hometown for more than ten years, decided she wanted to move back home. During the nine months that she spent looking for a job in Cincinnati, she sent her resume to fifteen places—a mix of corporate, association, and nonprofit positions. In her cover letter, she indicated that she would pay for face-to-face interviews, and ended up getting five of them. Out of the five in-person interviews she received, she ended up with three job offers.

A senior meeting planner in the Midwest found that "...unless the job came to me as a referral or through a headhunter it's more difficult to get your resume put on the top of the pile. I recently had an employer tell me she had pulled my resume because I had great qualifications, but due to my location put it on the bottom of the short list. It becomes very frustrating, because if I'm willing to relocate myself I'd at least like the opportunity for a phone interview. After the phone interview and learning a little more about the company and the position either party might not be interested or become more interested in the candidate." This candidate recently drove from Minneapolis to Chicago for an interview. As a result, she received an invitation to the association's headquarters in New York City for a final round of interviews.

In your cover letter, consider suggesting an initial phone interview in addition to offering to pay for an in-person interview. A phone interview is a good way for both parties—the employer and the job seeker—to determine whether the individual is a good prospect. For more tips on how to handle phone interviews, I recommend reading "Phone Interview Etiquette Can Propel You to the Next Step in the Hiring Process" found on Quintessential Careers Web site (www.quintcareers.com).

Offering to Pay to Relocate

Before you offer to pay for your relocation expenses, make certain you have an idea of what it is going to cost you to move to that new location. There are numerous sources on the Internet that can help you determine the cost of living in a new location. Some sites to check out are www.homefair.com/homefair/calc/salcalc.html, www.moving.com, www.cityrating.com, www.relocationapartments. com, and www.123relocation.com.

Negotiate When You Can

Negotiating contracts is an essential part of what we do as meeting professionals. As the meeting planner from Seattle realized, if part of her job involves negotiating contracts for her company or organization, then she should be able to negotiate reimbursement of some, if not all, of her relocation expenses. The key is to wait until they formally offer the job to you before beginning negotiating for assistance with relocation expenses. Decide in advance whether you will accept the position even if the employer declines to provide any assistance.

If You're Considering Relocating

Relocating to a new area is appealing, especially if it brings you closer to family and friends and includes less expensive housing/living expenses— even the opportunity to buy a home. When you're applying for jobs in other areas, it's important to establish a local presence; there are two ways you can do this without actually moving to the area. One is to set up a mailing address through a local UPS Store or other facility where you can "rent" an address. The second is to set up a voicemail box within the desired local area code.

If you are married or living with a partner, it's important to keep in mind how your decision to move to another part of the country affects his or her life. It is important to find out if a prospective employer has a policy about assisting an employee's spouse/partner with finding employment in the new location. Forty-two percent of the companies Atlas Van Lines surveyed in their study responded that they assist an employee's spouse/partner with finding employment in the new location.

Relocating involves careful consideration if you have children. You want to make sure that a new area has a school system of comparable quality to or better than the one where your children currently go to school. If your children are involved in sports, music, or other outside activities, you want to make sure that a new community offers a similar level of opportunities for them.

Interestingly, 62 percent of companies say that employees declined to relocate because of family issues or ties.

Housing

Also influencing an employee's relocation decision are the problems with the housing and mortgage markets. Fifty percent of respondents to the Atlas Van Lines survey say it is a primary reason an employee declined to relocate.

If you own a home, you will need to decide whether to sell or hold on to your residence. You should investigate what the market is like in the areas where you are considering moving. If the resale value of homes in a proposed relocation area is not as high as your current location, you could end up in worse financial shape. Some people hold on to their existing homes for the first six to twelve months to make certain that the new job works out. For one planner, keeping her current residence was a smart idea because shortly after she relocated, her new employer announced that the company was going through an acquisition and she was laid off.

Some companies will assist with paying your mortgage for a specific amount of time before turning over the sale of your home to a relocation company. According to the Employee Relocation Council (ERC), in 2006 two-thirds of companies offered to purchase an employee's home by outsourcing this through a home sale program. This level of assistance most often occurs with senior-level positions, such as a director or vice president of a department. For mid-range positions, about 20 percent of companies responded to the ERC's study that they would reimburse only for an employee's selling expenses.

If you don't own a home or plan to rent for a while, be sure to check out the rental opportunities in a new area. Can you find a comparable size apartment or home to rent that's within a reasonable commute zone to this new job? Will you need to pay for a storage unit if the place isn't large enough for all of your belongings?

Climate Changes

Weather, on the other hand, is a more serious consideration. In some parts of the country, seasons are less distinct and temperatures don't vary as dramatically as in other sections of the country. A meeting planner who moved from Orlando to Minneapolis said his first winter there was a real shock. When the first snowstorm hit, he called his office to leave word that he was not able to make it in because of the heavy snow in his driveway. He was surprised, and somewhat embarrassed, when his administrative assistant answered the phone because he knew she took the bus to work. When he inquired how she made it there on time, she reminded him that the weather was nothing new to her, and that in time, he would get used to it as well. This meeting planner not only learned how to accomplish his daily activities in a new climate, he quickly figured out how to readjust his thinking about planning programs in inclement weather.

Salaries

Salaries vary in different parts of the United States, as does the cost of living. Numerous Web sites provide cost of living comparisons. One that I like in particular is on a Web site called Homefair (www.homefair. com/cost of living/) because it not only offers a salary comparison, it also tells you how much you'd need to make to maintain your current standard of living. Here's an example of the kind of information this Web site provides.

Example (Created on www.homefair.com in March 2008): Suzanne, a meeting planner living in Santa Rosa, California, commutes to San Francisco to work in a large corporation's meeting planning department. She currently makes $75,000 per year and is interested in relocating to the East Coast. Suzanne wants to work in New York City but wants to live in Connecticut, preferably Stamford, Connecticut. Based on this information, this individual would need a salary of around $89,000 to match her current living expenses because the cost of living in Stamford is almost 19 percent higher than in Santa Rosa. Unfortunately, New York employers pay about 2.6 percent less than San Francisco, which means salaries for a comparable job pay approximately $73,000. Knowing there's a disparity between the salary and her living expenses, Suzanne might have to consider moving a bit further north toward Bridgeport, Connecticut, where living expenses are almost 12 percent less than in Santa Rosa, California. Even if her commute cost increased a bit, Suzanne could manage on a salary at around $66,000 because her overall living expenses are reduced.

Even if you're considering returning to an area where you grew up or previously lived, be sure to obtain as much information about the current economic situation in this location as possible. Look at professional association job boards to find out about the salaries offered in that area. Professional Convention Management Association (www.pcma.org) produces an annual salary survey that offers valuable information about salaries by job title and geographic area. In their 2007 salary survey, the average salary for a manager-level position on the West Coast paid $57,100 while it was only $55,500 on the East Coast. In a vice president position, the discrepancy was more noticeable with the average paid on the West Coast at $125,000 and only $112,500 on the East Coast.

Be sure to read the local newspapers online to find out about the housing market in the areas you're considering for relocation. If you have children, be sure to find out information about schools, hospitals, and other services your family may require. The local Chamber of Commerce is a great resource for this kind of information, as are certain Web sites such as Homefair, which also has a section called School Report.

Chapter Seven

ADDITIONAL WAYS TO SHOW YOUR ACCOMPLISHMENTS

There are two major misconceptions that hinder job seekers. One is that once they "get in the door" for an interview, they'll be able to provide more details about their experience and qualifications. With larger numbers of candidates applying for jobs online, the resume is the key to unlocking the door for an interview. Job seekers must clearly communicate their capabilities if they wish to stand out from the crowd.

The other misconception is that they are limited to a one-page resume—no matter how many years they have been planning meetings and events. The standard length for a resume these days is anywhere from one and a half to two pages. Having said that, two pages may still not provide enough room to highlight your meeting planning achievements.

Create an Addendum Page

Another way to provide a prospective employer with additional information about your qualifications is to create an addendum sheet that provides detailed information about the meetings and events you have managed. An addendum sheet is especially helpful if you've had a lengthy career or managed programs that included some unique elements, possibly because of the way you designed them or because the location of the event was such an unusual property, facility, or destination. While the resume includes particulars about the size and type of meetings, the addendum allows you to focus on these additional details. Here's an example of the type of information to include in an addendum page:

MEETING & SPECIAL EVENT SPECIFICS

- Approximately four face-to-face meetings for the national executive board.

  - Managed meetings that were usually 2–3 days in length for approximately forty to fifty people
  - Responsible for meetings held anywhere in the United States or Canada; three months' notice was typically given about desired meeting destinations
  - Created and oversaw the budget for all meetings
  - Was responsible for the booking of all travel and hotel accommodations for all meeting attendees
  - Worked with the choice hotel on banquet event orders and all necessary meeting arrangements (i.e., requests for special guests or senior staff, menus, evening cocktail parties, audio/visual).

- Annual Meeting

  - Managed meetings that rotated between Chicago, San Francisco, and New York with an average attendance between 250–750 people
  - Created and oversaw the budget
  - Responsible for the booking of all travel and hotel accommodations for all executive board, staff and special guests
  - Worked with the choice hotel on banquet event orders and all necessary meeting arrangements (i.e. requests for special guests or senior staff, menus, evening cocktail parties, audio/visual)
  - Interfaced with a committee of the host city on a cocktail party for approximately 150–200 members in the area.

Create a SALES Portfolio

Some people are more visually or tactilely oriented, so it's difficult for them to adequately process information if they only hear a description. These individuals operate more effectively when they can see or touch things. It's impossible to know in advance someone's learning orientation, which is the reason I recommend creating a "SALES" portfolio of your experience. "SALES" is an acronym for "Show All of your Experience and Capabilities Superbly."

One of the best ways to create a "SALES" portfolio is using an artist's portfolio in a binder format because it gives you the flexibility to add and replace sheets. The pages in this type of portfolio are usually black, which is a good background to highlight your information. Instead of pasting your information on the pages, consider using Velcro-type dots to attach your samples. This way, you can easily detach an item and let the interviewer look at and touch the piece of work.

Your SALES portfolio should include examples of your best work such as:

Marketing materials
Include samples of conference brochures, attendee registration forms, save the date postcards, e-cards for a trade show, or any other type of collateral that you had some hand in helping to design.

Special event materials
Managers like to see your creative side, so include copies of pieces such as an invitation to the company's gala awards dinner or an annual fundraiser, special menus for a VIP event, or welcome packets for an incentive. Even if you worked with a graphic designer to create a piece, include a sample so you can communicate how you managed the design project.

Forms and checklists

These documents show your ability to create methods for streamlining operations and managing meetings and events. These types of documents also provide a good way to lead into a discussion about how you use these forms as part of planning your meetings and events.

Photos of events and trade show booths

As the saying goes, "A picture is worth a thousand words," so include photos of special events, trade show booths, and general session productions. Make certain you use high-quality images.

A word of caution: Avoid placing your photos in plastic sleeves. One meeting planner did this and then left her SALES portfolio in her car for a week in the middle of summer, and the heat melted the plastic onto the photos. Unfortunately, she couldn't reproduce any of the images because the photos were of trade show booths she designed for a company that went bankrupt.

Chapter Eight

SAMPLE RESUMES

The samples in this chapter are designed to help give you a better understanding of the guidelines provided in Chapters Four and Five about crafting an effective resume. There are three resumes, each of which appears in two different versions. The first version represents the way the person originally put the resume together. The revised version includes detailed information about the person's experience and more effectively highlights his or her accomplishments and achievements. There are notes after each set of resumes to indicate the changes made.

The first resume reflects someone who held multiple positions with the same organization. She tried to keep to a one-page resume and as a result, shortchanged herself because she wasn't able to present the full scope of her experience and accomplishments.

The second resume was originally designed in a functional format. You can see how much more information you can provide in a chronological format about your background and experience.

The third resume is for someone who has reached a senior management position. The revised versions show how much easier it is to read the information when it's presented in a bulleted format instead of in paragraphs.

SAMPLE #1: MULTIPLE POSITIONS WITH ONE EMPLOYER *ORIGINAL VERSION*

MaryEllen Meechum

123 Cookie Dr., Chevy Chase, MD 20815

Home: 301.123.4567 * Cell: 301.765.4321 * memeechum@yahoo.com

Career Summary

Accomplished meetings director with extensive experience in planning, managing, and executing international conferences and events. Proven project management skills with exceptional problem-solving ability and strong attention to detail. Outstanding negotiator, communicator, and critical thinker with a background in implementing processes for change and growth while meeting external deadlines.

Professional Experience

Facial Reconstruction Institute (FRI)	**Chevy Chase, MD**
Director of Conferences – FRI	**May 2003 – Present**
Meeting Planner – FRI	**February 1998 – May 2003**

Fully accountable for long-term success of conference department. Report to executive director; work with executive committee, board of directors and network of volunteers; supervise conference staff.

- Execute multiple international technical conferences and events concurrently in different stages of development. Plan events domestically and internationally, including France and Taiwan
- Create long-range strategic goals and develop budget projections for three years into future. Increased revenue 30 percent over previous year while decreasing expenses through contract, food & beverage (f&b) and external vendor negotiations
- Develop program content with program chairs and committees. Interact with industry leaders for all aspects of conferences. Speaker management for over two hundred speakers
- Grew sponsor/vendor program 25 percent; established new levels of sponsorship to meet identified market needs
- Increased registration by 20 percent through aggressive marketing including design & development of call for papers, advance program, flyers, postcards, ad placement, & Web
- Produce comprehensive on-site materials including proceedings, technical digest/program, and registration materials
- On-site management including registration, f&b, audio-visual, and risk management
- Source all aspects of program including hotel, venue site selection, contract negotiation, AV, off-site events, and other vendor partnerships
- Highly proficient in MS Office, Adobe Acrobat, Quark XPress (PC & Mac).

Education & Professional Development

B.S., Hotel & Lodging Management

Johnson & Wales University, Providence, RI

Member of AAFPS (American Academy of Facial Plastic Surgery)

SAMPLE #2: MULTIPLE POSITIONS WITH ONE EMPLOYER *REVISED VERSION*
MaryEllen Meechum, CMP
123 Cookie Dr., Chevy Chase, MD 20815
Home: 301.123.4567 * Cell: 301.765.4321
memeechum@yahoo.com

Career Summary
As an accomplished meetings director, successfully plan and execute international conferences and events. Outstanding negotiator, strategic planner, and critical thinker, creating solutions to issues related to attendee and organizational growth.

Professional Experience
Facial Reconstruction Institute (FRI),   4/98 – Present
Chevy Chase, MD
Director of Conferences (5/03 – Present)
- Responsible for executing four technical conferences each year—three with ancillary events in the United States and one biannual international conference
- Develop three-year budget projections and create long-range strategic goals for conferences focusing on avenues to elevate the level of topics and expand attendance
- Prepared a business plan resulting in the institute's launch of an international conference. Since 2004, successfully operated two in France, and a third is scheduled in Taiwan (2008) including a one-day pre-conference
- Revenue increased over 23 percent to $494,527 in 2007 for one event by decreasing expenses through effective contract negotiations related to food and beverage, hotel and external vendor negotiations
- Sponsorship revenue increased in 2007 by 25 percent to $81,900 and exhibitor revenue by 28 percent to $116,115. Established new sponsorship program to meet marketing needs identified by sponsors; new sponsorship areas include student paper award, printing of the technical digest, awards luncheon, and speaker appreciation breakfast
- Created an aggressive marketing plan in 2007 producing a 25 percent increase in registration from 380 to 475 attendees
- Initiated green meetings policy for conferences coordinating with hotels on recycling including paper usage and bulk consumption of food and beverage
- Continually exploring ways to expand food and beverage functions for the conference to increase the value and networking opportunities for attendees
- Focus on enhancing the registration process and materials, establishing more procedures related to risk management
- Handle all aspects of contract negotiations and review with the Institute's legal counsel
- Develop content with program chairs and committees, interacting with industry leaders on all aspects of the conferences
- Work with a graphic designer to create the call for papers, advance program, flyers, postcards, ad placement & Web site. Responsible for proofreading all copy and overseeing the print production process
- Coordinate two board of director meetings per year and assist with coordinating four executive committee meetings. Responsible for reporting to board of directors about accomplishments with the strategic plan
- Supervise two full-time staff—a meeting coordinator and administrative assistant—and one contractor, a graphic designer.

Meeting Planner (4/98 – 3/01)
- Responsible for managing over two hundred presenters from twenty-seven countries at the annual conference; established the speaker schedule for five concurrent tracks over four days
- Interfaced with high-level industry professionals including PhDs, laser physicists, engineers, and CEOs of member organizations regarding content for conferences
- Designed the call for papers, advance program, flyers, postcards, and other marketing materials using desktop publishing software
- Produced comprehensive on-site materials including proceedings, technical digest, conference program, and registration materials
- On-site management of conferences including meeting room setup, food and beverage functions, table top vendor show, audio-visual requirements, and risk management
- Developed menus that are sensitive to the varied dietary needs of attendees (50 percent of attendees are from international locations)
- Sourced all aspects of the programs including hotel and venue site selection, contract negotiations, audio visual, off-site events, and vendor partnerships.

Education
B.S., Hotel & Lodging Management, Johnson & Wales University, Providence, RI

Certified Meeting Professional (CMP), Convention Industry Council   2008

Professional Affiliation
Member, American Academy of Facial Plastic Surgery (AAFPS)   2004-Present

Computer Skills
Highly proficient on both PC & Mac using MS Word, Excel, PowerPoint, Outlook, IMIS, FilemakerPro, Adobe Acrobat, and Quark XPress

Notes: In the original version, by attempting to keep to a one-page resume, MaryEllen had to eliminate a lot of information about her qualifications and experience with both positions. She wasn't able to identify the expanded responsibilities she had as director of conferences. The revised version allowed her to highlight accomplishments with both positions she held, and she was still able to fit it into a one-and-one-quarter-page resume format.

SAMPLE #3: FUNCTIONAL FORMAT *ORIGINAL VERSION*
Sandy Sunshine
333 Frosty Rd., Palo Alto, CA 94404 (650) 123-4567 ssunshine@comcast.net

Objective

A leadership position in event and meeting management in a dynamic and innovative environment.

Skills

- Substantial project management experience
- Ability to manage multiple projects and objectives simultaneously with a variety of deadlines occurring within the same time frame
- Managed, trained, and developed staff members, including on-site support staff
- Able to work independently or as a team player
- Analytically minded, able to think strategically and respond tactically
- Excellent verbal, written, and interpersonal skills.

Summary of Experience

Conference/Event Management Experience

- Managed logistics, time lines, budgets, site selection, billing, vendor negotiations and contracts, decorators, speakers, exhibitors, transportation, off-site/on-site events, entertainment, registration, audiovisual equipment, space arrangements/allocations, hotel contracts, housing, and food/beverage for multicity road show, association, board of directors, executive committee, sales, user, and partner conferences with 300-7,000 attendees
- Coordinated logistics including supplies, stage, decorations, audiovisual equipment, awards, food/beverage, and security issues for a four-day event with 2,000 government and private sector attendees
- Planned and provided tactical support for all aspects of trade shows including shipping, set-ups and tear downs, staffing, schedules, demonstrations, and media kit assembly
- Managed logistics, served as secretary, and acted as support staff, for a local cycling team.

Marketing Experience

- Designed and developed specialized promotional materials
- Produced newsletter articles that reached 3,500 staff members
- Managed promotional photo shoot with results used for development of Web site-based marketing campaign and promotions
- Collaborated with business development staff to identify key prospects for co-branding relationships.

Employment History

XYZ HOTEL COMPANY	SAN JOSE, CA
Meetings and Special Events Manager	2004 to 2007
Bubble Research Center (Contractor)	UNION CITY, CA
Event Manager	2003 to 2004
	1999 to 2000

M. Sotherby & Associates   BERKELEY, CA
Convention & Meetings Manager   2002 to 2003

ABC Planners Group   FREMONT, CA
Project Manager   2000 to 2001

M-Class, Incorporated   MOUNTAIN VIEW, CA
Business Development Project Manager   1998 to 1999

XYZ Worldwide Books (contractor)   SOUTH SAN FRANCISCO, CA
Event Marketing Coordinator   1998 to 1998

VISA USA   FOSTER CITY, CA
Senior Analyst/Auditor   1992 to 1997

Education and Licenses

San Francisco State University   **San Francisco, CA**
- B.S. in Business Administration with a Marketing concentration   1999
- Certified Meeting Planner (CMP) Designation   In Progress

Computer Skills and Affiliations

- Proficient with Microsoft Office Suite (Word, Excel, and PowerPoint), Microsoft Project, Windows Vista/XP/ME/2007/2000/98/95/NT and most other standard business software applications
- Volunteer, ABC Foundation
- Volunteer, T Sports Inc.

SAMPLE RESUMES

SAMPLE #4: FUNCTIONAL FORMAT *CONVERTED TO CHRONOLOGICAL*
Sandy Sunshine
333 Frosty Rd., Palo Alto, CA 94404
Ph: (650) 123-4567
E-mail: ssunshine@comcast.net

Summary of Experience
XYZ Hotel Company, San Jose, CA   **7/04 to 12/07**
Meetings and Special Events Manager

- Managed logistics for an outdoor music event held 2–3 times per year for about 300 people per concert. Held in conjunction with local jazz radio station, this event included coordinating food and beverage stations and VIP areas.
- Serviced 10–15 group events per month with 10 – 300 persons for companies in the high-tech, biotech, Internet, banking and securities industries, venture capital, and nonprofit organizations.
- Programs managed included fundraising events such as casino nights, silent and live auctions, plated awards dinners and banquets, education seminars, executive board meetings, sales meetings, and a Lamborghini customer drive
- Coordinated food and beverage for client programs, working closely with the executive chef and staff to create menus that addressed gourmet as well as special dietary needs
- Prepared, distributed, and revised banquet event orders and conference resumes
- Successfully managed vendor relationships in relation to client requirements for audio visual, floral, décor, transportation, specialty linens, pipe and drape for exhibits, and off-site activities
- Trained new meeting and special event coordinators about hotel policies and procedures.

Bubble Research Center, Union City, CA
Event Manager (Various contract or assignments) 1999 – 2000 and 2003 – 2004

- Assisted with coordinating seminars and other 1-2 day meetings for the Risk Analysis Department
- Orchestrated Safety and Quality Week for employees that included educational courses and culminated with a Chili Cook-off and Awards Ceremony
- Coordinated a committee comprised of professionals from 10-12 internal departments who acted as liaisons regarding areas their department would contribute to the program
- Produced a newsletter and articles about this special program that went out to 3,000 employees
- Worked with keynote speaker, Jim Lovell, arranging all of his travel arrangements
- Responsible for coordinating the Safety and Quality Department's participation in the Shuttle Space Development Conference held at Moffitt Field. Produced displays for their trade show booth and managed set-up the day of the show

M. Sotherby & Associates, Berkeley, CA   **2002 – 2003**
Convention & Meetings Manager

- Responsible for managing all logistics for the quarterly board of directors meetings for the West Coast chapter of an orthodontic and dentist association
- Managed up to twenty-four 2–3 day continuing education seminars for dental support staff. Handled registration, confirmed exhibitors for tabletop trade show (20–25 per seminar), arranged all meal functions, meeting space logistics, and worked with speakers on travel arrangements and presentations
- Assisted with the site inspection, contract negotiations with the exhibit service contractor, and destination management company for the association's annual conference. Between 1,700–2,200 people attended this weeklong conference

ABC Planners Group, Fremont, CA   **5/00 – 5/01**
Project Manager
- Managed logistics, time lines, budgets, site selection, billing, vendor negotiations and contracts, decorators, speakers, exhibitors, transportation, off-site/on-site events, entertainment, registration, audiovisual equipment, space arrangements/allocations, hotel contracts, housing, and food/beverage for multi-city road show, sales, user, and partner conferences with 300–7,000 attendees
- Liaised with corporate clients about implementing their meeting specifications. Clients were primarily high-tech and venture capital companies based in the San Francisco Bay Area
- Coordinated logistics including decor, audiovisual equipment, awards, food and beverage, and security issues for a four day event with 2,000 government and private sector attendees
- Planned and provided tactical support for all aspects of trade shows including shipping, set-ups and tear downs, staffing, schedules, demonstrations, and media kit assembly.

M-Class Incorporated, Mountain View, CA   **1998 – 1999**
Business Development Project Manager
- Responsible for trade show coordination of 8 × 10 booths including booth design, set-up and tear-down at 12 shows
- Designed and developed specialized promotional materials
- Managed promotional photo shoot with results used for development of Web site-based marketing campaign and promotions
- Collaborated with business development staff to identify key prospects for co-branding relationships.

XYZ Worldwide Books, South San Francisco, CA   **1998 – 1998**
Event Marketing Coordinator (Contract Assignment)
- Supported Event Manager with follow-up on event details
- Shipped conference materials

EDUCATION
B.S., Business Administration, San Francisco State University, San Francisco, CA
(Marketing Concentration)
Certified Meeting Professional (CMP) designation

VOLUNTEER INVOLVEMENT
ABC Foundation, San Francisco, CA   **2001 – Present**
- Assist at the annual fundraiser event that occurs over once a year in Monterey. Help with the live and silent auctions and coordinate transportation for attendees from designated hotels to the event

Volunteer, T Sports LLC, Berkeley, CA   **2000 – 2003**
- Acted as the course marshal for annual bike races and helped in the media booth issuing badges to media at the race

Computer Skills and Affiliations
- Proficient with MSWord, Excel, PowerPoint, Microsoft Project, and other standard business software applications

NOTES: With Sandy's resume in a functional format, it was difficult to determine whether the work she noted happened in recent years or ten years ago. She was also unable to provide as much detail about her experience and accomplishments under the two categories. Converting this into a chronological format allowed Sandy to provide the type of details about her experience that employers typically seek—length of programs and number of attendees—and the types of meetings, events, and trade shows she's managed.

SAMPLE RESUMES

SAMPLE #5 – SENIOR MANAGEMENT RESUME *ORIGINAL VERSION*
Frank Horn, CMP
1 Fremont Street, Seattle, Washington 98109
(206) 123-4567

SKILLS SUMMARY

- **Extensive leadership experience, including**
  - o   Executive team, corporate board, and nonprofit management
  - o   Facilitative meeting management
  - o   Large team management including staff coaching and performance management.

- **Broad meeting and event industry experience, including**
  - o   Strategic meeting management program development
  - o   Incentives, conferences, board and leadership meetings
  - o   Corporate and 3rd party planning, and hotel administration.

- **Strong customer satisfaction record, including**
  - o   ROI/ROO through objective-based meeting planning, cost savings and avoidance
  - o   Customer satisfaction survey results that meet and exceed expectations
  - o   Development of technology tools for registration, scheduling, planning and reporting

Senior Leadership

Director of Staff, ABC Company   **2004 – 2006**

Reported to the president of the company to oversee the effective operation of the senior leadership team; managed company's relationships with critical stakeholders including the board of directors and holding company; and worked directly with the president on a variety of issues, policies and strategies, including internal and external communications plans. Oversight for company's conferences and events, overall corporate calendar management, and scheduling.

Corporate Meeting Planning

Director, Corporate Events, ABC Company   **2006 – present**

Realigned the Corporate Events group as a strategic meeting management organization focusing on objective-based planning, branding, messaging, return-on-investment, and the benefits of centralized sourcing: delivered quality assurance, risk management, and tracked cost savings and avoidance. The staff of seven planners manages both internal meetings such as international incentive trips, conferences, and board meetings, as well as external sponsorship and consumer revenue-generating events.

Events Department tracked millions of dollars in savings and cost avoidance to the enterprise through strategic sourcing. Internal clients gave department highest marks for meeting or exceeding expectations in achieving event objectives. Produced thousands of leads and direct revenue to the sales organization from branded consumer events.

Developed intranet site with self-service tools and coaching to move post-contract planning logistics for small meetings to the businesses allowing event staff to focus on sourcing, planning and strategic influence on larger high-impact conferences.

Senior Meeting Planner, ABC Company   **2002 – 2004**

Provided company-wide meeting and event services. Client base included the senior leadership team, board of directors, and the sales organization. Brought professionally managed events, documented savings, and consolidation practices to the company. Heavy emphasis on vendor and industry relationships, and contract ethics and negotiations. Joined newly formed department at its inception and worked collaboratively to grow department policies, processes and staff to support steadily increasing business including a series of incentive and annual meetings formerly contracted to an external vendor. Selected vendor and implemented processes for Web-based registration for attendee registration and surveys. Created Outlook-based events calendar as a scheduling and resource-management tool. Developed department intranet site.

Project Manager, XYZ Events Company   **2001 – 2002**

Managed conference operations for small event planning company focusing on revenue-generating meetings. Managed sponsor and speaker coordination and correspondence, Web registration, and event planning operations. Coordinated a series of professionally produced teleconferences including speaker recruitment, minute-to-minute script writing, and technology vendor management.

Manager, Meeting Planning, Axel Manufacturing Company   **1998 – 2001**

Supervised team of 10 meeting planners located across the country and contributed as lead West coast planner for company's travel and meeting management group, providing global meetings support. Responsible for scheduling meeting planners and contractors for over 500 meetings annually. Actively participated on the leadership team in creating policy and procedure to integrate travel and meeting services. Created quantitative team performance objectives linked directly to department goals of cost savings and client service.

Coordinated vendor selection and implementation of a Web-based registration product to force compliance with airline partner discounts. Worked closely with designated travel agency to coordinate discounted and zone airfares. Initiated and managed relationships and contracts with external suppliers including DMCs, production and transportation companies, speakers, entertainers, meeting technology resource suppliers, and managers of off-site facilities.

Meetings and Events Manager, Grocery Chain   **1993 – 1998**

Managed the Meetings and Events department for company's Northern California office managing client focused events, meetings, conferences employee recognition events and community sponsorship fulfillment. Supervised staff coordinator and project-based contractors and consultants. Designed and maintained department intranet site featuring a dynamic calendar of meetings and events for company scheduling, and a database for event registration.

Hotel and University Catering and Convention Services
Director of Catering and Convention Services   **1991 – 1993**
Hotel #1, Washington, WA
Director of Catering, Hotel #2, Seattle, WA   **1988 – 1991**
Catering Manager, Hotel #3, Berkeley, CA   **1986 – 1988**
Conference Manager, University of California,   **1984 – 1986**
Berkeley, CA

Appointments and Affiliations
Certified Meeting Professional (CMP)   **2000**
Meeting Professionals International (MPI)   **1994 – present**
Seattle Chapter
Held various positions on chapter's board of directors including vice president positions and
chair of various committees
National Association of Catering Directors (NACE)   **1988 – 1993**
Seattle Chapter
Served on board of directors and committee work

Education
Bachelor of Arts in Business Management
San Francisco State University, San Francisco, CA   June 1984

SAMPLE #6: SENIOR MANAGEMENT RESUME *REVISED VERSION*
Frank Horn, CMP
1 Fremont Street, Seattle, WA 98109
(206) 123-4567
e-mail: frank.horn@gmail.com

Skills Summary

- **Extensive leadership experience, including:**
  - o Executive team, corporate board, and nonprofit management
  - o Trained in facilitative meeting management
  - o Direct and event team management
- **Broad meeting industry experience, including:**
  - o Corporate and third-party planning, hotel catering and convention services
  - o Strategic meeting management program development
  - o International incentives, conferences, board and leadership meetings.

ABC Company, Seattle, WA   2003 – present
Director Corporate Events (2006 – Present)

- Promoted to realign department as a strategic meeting management organization. Responsible for leveraging the benefits of centralized sourcing from site selection to contracting, quality assurance, risk management, tracked spend, savings and cost avoidance, and objective-based meeting planning, branding, messaging, and return-on-investment for over 250 meetings annually with groups ranging in size from 50–2,500 participants
- Oversee operations and manage five staff members who plan internal board/executive meetings, conferences, and international incentives, as well as external consumer lead- and revenue-generating events. Align individual performance and department goals with enterprise strategy
- Developed intranet site with self-service tools and coaching to move post-contract planning logistics for small meetings to the businesses so event staff can focus on sourcing, and strategic planning of large high-impact meetings.

Director of Staff (2004 – 2006)

- Promoted to report directly to the president to oversee the effective operation of the company's senior leadership team, managing relationships with critical stakeholders including the board of directors, and holding company
- Oversaw company's conferences and events, overall corporate calendar management, and scheduling
- Worked directly with the president on a variety of issues, policies and strategies, including internal and external communications plans.

Senior Meeting Planner (2002 – 2004)

- Established executive meeting management and consolidation practices such as contract clauses and documented cost savings to the company at the inception of its corporate events department. Worked collaboratively to grow department policies, processes, and staff to support increasing business
- Converted a series of incentive and annual meetings from an external planner to in-house management
- Provided meeting and event services to the senior leadership team, board of directors, and the sales organization
- Selected vendor and implemented processes for Web-based registration for attendee registration and surveys. Created Outlook-based events calendar as a scheduling, tracking, and resource-management tool; and co-created department intranet site marketing our products and services to the company.

XYZ Events Company, San Rafael, CA   **2001 – 2002**
(contract assignment) Operations Manager
- Managed conference operations ranging in size from 250–5,000 attendees for event planning company focusing on revenue-generating meetings
- Handled sponsor and speaker coordination and correspondence, Web registration, and event planning operations
- Coordinated professionally produced teleconferences including speaker recruitment, script writing, and technology vendor management.

Axel Manufacturing Company, Mountain View, CA   **1998 – 2001**
Manager Meeting Planning (2001 – 2002)
Senior Meeting Planner (1999 – 2001)
- Managed virtual team of 10 meeting planners located across the country and contributed as West Coast lead planner for company's travel and meeting management group, providing global meetings support to all firm service lines
- Responsible for internal meeting planners and contractors for over 500 meetings annually using a proprietary database tool that first secured electronic sign-off from meeting budget holders
- Actively participated leadership team to create policies and procedures integrating travel and meeting services
- Created quantitative team performance goals aligned to department goals of cost savings and client service
- Co-coordinated vendor selection and implementation of a Web-based registration tool to force compliance with the firm's airline partner discounts and travel policies

Grocery Chain, San Francisco, CA   **1993 – 1998**
Meetings and Events Manager
- Managed the Meetings and Events department for company's Northern California office
- Planned approximately 1,000 client focused and employee recognition events, meetings, conferences, and community sponsorship fulfillment. Events ranged in size from 150–10,000 participants
- Designed department intranet site featuring a calendar of events for company scheduling, and a database for event registration
- Supervised one staff coordinator as well as project-based contractors and consultants.

Hotel Catering and Convention Experience
Director of Catering and Convention Services Hotel, Los Angeles, CA   1990 – 1992

Appointments and Affiliations
Certified Meeting Professional (CMP)   2000
Meeting Professionals International (MPI)
Northern California Chapter   1993 – present
National Association of Catering Directors (NACE)   1989 – 1992
Los Angeles Chapter

Education
B.A., Business Management, San Francisco State University, San Francisco, CA

NOTES: Hiring managers typically spend up to twenty seconds initially scanning a resume. When you put your information in paragraphs, as Frank did in the original version of his resume, it slows down the reader so that he or she is less likely to get all the way through your resume. In the revised version using bullets, it's much easier to catch the salient points about Frank's experience.

Frank also presented the three positions he held at ABC Company separately, so it appeared at first glance that they were with different companies and that he wasn't in each position for more than two years. By listing the company and the total number of years Frank has been with the company, a prospective employer can see that he's actually been with ABC Company for five years. Each position notes the number of years he held it so that a prospective employer can also see his growth within the company.

It's also important to note that although both versions include Hotel Catering and Convention Experience, the revised version shows only one position. The average length of time to present on a resume is ten to twelve years unless there's other relevant experience that goes back further than that. Although it's best not to exceed fifteen years, Frank felt it was important to show that he has a background includes working on the hospitality side of the industry.